# TREASURY MANAGEMENT

CW00832687

# THE FINANCIAL SKILLS SERIES

The rapidly changing role of the finance function in modern organizations is creating greater and more varied demands on the skills of everyone involved in the world of finance and accounting. To enable busy professionals to keep up with the pace of change, Kogan Page has joined forces with the Chartered Institute of Management Accountants (CIMA) to create an up-to-the-minute series of books on financial skills.

Highly practical in nature, each book is packed with expert advice and information on a specific financial skill, while the lively style adopted reflects the current dynamism of the discipline.

**Published titles in the series include:**

*Cost Control: A Strategic Guide*
David Doyle

*Financial Modelling for Business Decisions*
Bryan Kefford

*Financial Planning*
*Modelling Methods and Techniques*
Second edition
David Asch and G Roland Kaye

*Financial Planning Using Spreadsheets*
*Forecasting, Planning & Budgeting Techniques*
Sue Nugus

*Implementing an Accounting System*
*A Practical Guide*
Revised edition
Ray Franks

*An Introduction to Strategic Financial Management*
*The Key to Long-Term Profitability*
David Allen

*Investment Appraisal*
*A Guide for Managers*
Second edition
Rob Dixon

*Measuring Corporate Performance*
M Broadbent

*A Practical Guide to Activity-Based Costing*
Falconer Mitchell and John Innes

*A Practical Guide to Target Costing*
*Processes and Techniques*
Frank Robinson

*Quality in the Finance Function*
David Lynch

*Strategic Financial Decisions*
David Allen

For further information on the series, please contact the Marketing department at Kogan Page, 120 Pentonville Road, London N1 9JN (tel: 0171 278 0433; fax 0171 837 6348). CIMA members can also contact the Publishing Department at the Institute.

# TREASURY MANAGEMENT

## TOOLS AND TECHNIQUES FOR COUNTERING FINANCIAL RISKS

*John Ogilvie*

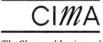

The Chartered Institute of
Management Accountants

**KOGAN**
**PAGE**

First published 1999

Apart from any fair dealing for the purposes of research or private study, or criticism or review, as permitted under the Copyright, Designs and Patents Act 1988, this publication may only be reproduced, stored or transmitted, in any form or by any means, with the prior permission in writing of the publishers, or in the case of reprographic reproduction in accordance with the terms and licences issued by the CLA. Enquiries concerning reproduction outside these terms should be sent to the publishers at the undermentioned address:

Kogan Page Limited
120 Pentonville Road
London N1 9JN

© John Ogilvie, 1999

The right of John Ogilvie to be identified as the author of this work has been asserted by him in accordance with the Copyright, Designs and Patents Act 1988.

**British Library Cataloguing in Publication Data**

A CIP record for this book is available from the British Library.

ISBN 0 7494 1310 7

Typeset by The Florence Group, Stoodleigh, Devon
Printed and bound by Clays Ltd, St Ives plc

# Contents

# Preface

Treasury management activities are undertaken in all organizations. In larger organizations the function of treasury management is sufficiently significant as to warrant a treasury specialism within the finance function.

The development of a specialized treasury department has essentially been in response to the increased number of risks faced by organizations in today's business world, and the greater range of products or techniques available to counter those risks.

This book sets out the role and activities of the treasury manager and considers a range of treasury management techniques and tools. Many of these techniques and tools are, by their nature, very technical. Here we seek to provide a comprehensive overview of treasury management in a way that will enable the activities and techniques to be understood by both finance specialists and those who are not employed within the finance function. The focus is to provide an insight into the techniques of treasury management and provide an explanation of how they may be of use to the treasury manager. It is intended to complement other texts within the *Financial Skills Series*, which cover such topics as financial management and investment appraisal.

# 1

# Introduction to Treasury Management

The precise structure and role of the finance function within an organization will vary according to such factors as its size, the nature of its business, and the complexity of its organizational structure. However, within any organization, the finance function will be responsible for the provision and management of financial resources.

The establishment of a specialist treasury function within the finance department can be traced back to the late 1960s. Developments in technology, the breakdown of exchange controls, increasing volatility in interest and exchange rates, combined with the increasing globalization of business, have all contributed to greater opportunities and risks for businesses over the last three decades. To survive in today's complex financial environment, businesses need to be able to actively manage both their ability to undertake these opportunities, and their exposure to risks.

Businesses have needed to become more aware of the expanding range of hybrid capital instruments (eg convertible preference shares issued in the name of a subsidiary registered in the Dutch Antilles) and financial instruments (forward markets and the various derivatives markets) and to be able to select from these the ones which are appropriate to the businesses' needs in the prevailing circumstances. A separate treasury function is more likely to develop the appropriate skills, and it should also be easier to achieve economies of scale; for instance, in achieving lower borrowing rates, or netting-off balances.

## KEY DECISION AREAS

The activities of the finance function may be grouped together into three key decision areas to reflect the responsibilities of providing financial resources and managing those resources. These key decision areas are investment, financing and dividend:

1.  *Investment decisions* are those which determine how scarce resources in terms of funds available are committed to projects, which can range from acquiring a piece of plant to the acquisition of another entity. Investing in fixed assets usually carries the need for supporting investment in working capital, eg stocks and debtors, fewer creditors, an aspect often not properly taken into account by management. Investment to enhance internal growth is often called 'internal investment' as compared with acquisitions, which represent 'external investment'.

    The other side of the investment coin is *disinvestment*, which means the preparedness to withdraw from unsuccessful projects, and the disposal of parts of an entity which no longer fit with the parent entity's strategy. Such decisions usually involve one very special element – the right timing for the action to be taken.

    Disinvestment decisions can also be involved in reconstructions whereby an entity has to alter its capital structure, possibly to survive as a result of grievous losses.

2.  *Financing decisions* relate to acquiring the optimum finance to meet financial objectives and seeing that fixed and working capital are effectively managed. The financial manager needs to possess a good knowledge of the sources of available funds and their respective costs, and needs to ensure that the entity has a sound capital structure, ie a proper balance between equity capital and debt. Such managers also need to have a very clear understanding as to the difference between profit and cash flow, bearing in mind that profit is of little avail unless the entity is adequately supported by

cash to pay for assets and sustain the working capital cycle. Financing decisions also call for a good knowledge of evaluation of risk, eg excessive debt carries high risk for an entity's equity because of the priority rights of the lenders. A major area for risk-related decisions is in overseas trading where an entity is vulnerable to currency fluctuations, and the manager must be well aware of the various protective procedures such as *hedging* available.

3. *Dividend decisions* relate to the determination as to how much and how frequently cash can be paid out of the profits of an entity as income for its proprietors. The owner of any profit-making organization looks for reward for investment in two ways, the growth of the capital invested and the cash paid out as income; for a sole trader this income would be termed 'drawings' and for a limited liability company the term is 'dividends'.

   The dividend decision thus has two elements: the amount to be paid out and the amount to be retained to support the growth of the entity, the latter being also a financing decision; the level and regular growth of dividends represent a significant factor in determining a profit-making company's market value, ie the value placed on its shares by the stock market.

All three types of decision are interrelated, and cannot be considered in isolation. However, as an organization increases in size the responsibilities of the finance function are likely to be subdivided, broadly in line with these three decision areas, into two main functions or departments, namely treasury and financial control.

This book will focus on treasury management, which is concerned with raising finance, management of liquid resources, management of currency and interest rate risks, and management of relationships with banks.

## ROLE OF THE TREASURER

The treasury function exists in every business, though in small businesses it may form part of a department covering other functions, such as accounting or company secretarial work. In a larger company, it is likely to be a separate department reporting to the chief financial officer, but communications with the rest of the organization need to be in good order if an effective service is to be provided.

*Treasury* is concerned with the relationship between the entity and its financial stakeholders, which include shareholders, fund lenders and taxation authorities, while *financial control* provides the relationship with other stakeholders such as customers, suppliers and employees.

In larger companies and groups, treasury will usually be centralized at head office, providing a service to all the various units of the entity and thereby achieving economies of scale, eg by obtaining better borrowing rates, whereas financial control is now frequently delegated to individual units, where it can more closely impact on customers and suppliers and relate more specifically to the competition which those units have to face. As a result, treasury and financial control may often tend to be separated by location as well as by responsibilities.

The main functions of the treasurer can be classified as:

- *Banking* The treasurer will be responsible for managing relationships with the banks. In this book this function is viewed as an integral part of the three other functions identified below, and is considered within the chapters covering those specific functions.
- *Liquidity management* This will involve working capital and money management. The treasurer will need to ensure that the business has the liquid funds it needs, and invest surplus funds.
- *Funding management* Funding management is concerned with identifying suitable sources of funds which requires

knowledge of the sources available, the cost of those sources, whether any security is required, and management of interest rate risks.

- *Currency management*   The treasurer would be responsible for providing the business with forecasts of exchange rate movements which, in turn, will determine the procedures adopted to manage exchange rate risks. Dealing in the foreign exchange markets and day-to-day management of foreign exchange risks becomes a key function for the treasurer.

The treasurer's key tasks can also be categorized according to the three levels of management:

1. *strategic*, eg matters concerning the capital structure of the business and distribution/retention policies, the actual raising of capital, including share issues, the assessment of the likely return from each source and the appropriate proportions of funds from each source, the decision as to the level of dividends, and consideration of alternative forms of finance;
2. *tactical*, eg the management of cash/investments and decisions as to the hedging of currency or interest rate risk;
3. *operational*, eg the transmission of cash, placing of 'surplus' cash and other dealings with banks.

Treasurers require specialist skills to be able to handle effectively an ever-growing range of capital instruments, eg convertible preference shares issued in the name of an offshore subsidiary, and to determine the most suitable way to protect their company from foreign exchange risk, which demands a good knowledge of forward markets and an ability to select the most appropriate methods of hedging and foreign exchange cover. They also need a knowledge of taxation in all areas in which the group operates and, deriving from that, the ability to advise effectively on policies such as transfer pricing in permissible ways to minimize overall tax liability, and to be able to liaise competently with the group taxation department.

The capacity to make large gains or losses is enormous: a treasurer can wipe out, in a few hours, all the profit made from making and selling things over several months. It is important, therefore, that authority and responsibility associated with the treasury function are carefully defined and monitored. This becomes even more important as the range of derivatives increases. Senior managers need to be aware of which risks are being carried, which laid off, and, where appropriate, taken on. There is also growing pressure for companies to disclose, in their annual reports, more information about their treasury policies, and their 'positions' as at the balance sheet date.

Both the treasurer and the financial controller will usually be responsible to the finance director, whose concern will be to harmonize their activities in an efficient manner.

Examples comparing their relationships are:

1. the treasurer is best able to assess cost of capital and quantify the entity's aversion to risk, while the financial controller relates these factors to group strategy;
2. the financial controller identifies the entity's currency risks, while the treasurer advises on the best means to hedge the risks.

### Cost centre or profit centre

An area for debate is whether the treasury activities should be accounted for simply as a cost centre, or as a business in its own right, seeking to make a profit out of its activities, eg by charging other businesses in the enterprise for its services (and giving those businesses the choice of whether they use it or a bank).

As indicated above, the case for a separation of treasury – not only from accounting but also from financial control – is a strong one. The question remains, however, as to how its performance/ progress should be measured/assessed.

Some people would argue for a 'profit centre' approach. This usually means that the treasury charges individual business units a market rate for the service it provides. If it writes currency options, for example, it charges the business unit a premium in line with that charged by the banks. It then has the task of managing that option (by buying and selling in the forward market, or by using derivatives) for a cost which leaves it with a profit. The main argument for this is that the treasurer is then motivated to do what is best for the company as a whole, ie to minimize the cost of the operation. Spot checks are obviously required (eg by internal audit) to ensure that charges are indeed at market rates, since there is an imbalance in the amount of information available to the two parties (weighted in favour of the treasurers).

There are obviously some administrative costs involved, but the main drawback in practice has been that some treasurers have interpreted the profit concept as encouraging them to speculate. If it can make a profit from writing options, why not write them for other companies? If it understands the foreign currency markets, why not speculate, eg swap funds from currencies expected to depreciate into those expected to appreciate? Often spectacular gains can be made, but the record shows that spectacular losses are at least as likely. A sound internal control system is a necessity in any treasury function, but especially so when speculation is encouraged.

Consequently, there are many who advocate a 'cost centre' approach. This usually means that the costs of running the department are collected (and, no doubt, compared with budget) but that the substance of the transactions which they manage is reflected in the business unit's books, eg the 'profit' made on writing options is credited to the business for which it was written. Alternatively, the profits/losses are allowed to lie where they fall: eg the business unit carries the profit or loss on an overseas sale (according to the spot rate when the cash is received) and the treasury carries the offsetting currency loss/gain respectively (the difference between the forward rate obtained and the eventual spot rate). This approach collects the total cost/benefit of hedging. It discourages speculation but may, by the same token, discourage initiative. Confrontation can occur when the business unit bears a loss, caused – as it sees it – by the treasury.

In summary, the main advantages of operating treasury as a profit centre rather than as a cost centre are:

- individual business units of the entity can be charged a market rate for the service provided, thereby making their operating costs more realistic;
- the treasurer is motivated to provide services as effectively and economically as possible to ensure that a profit is made at the market rate, eg in managing hedging activities for a subsidiary, thereby benefiting the group as a whole.

The main disadvantages are:

- the profit concept is a temptation to speculate, eg by swapping funds from currencies expected to depreciate into those expected to appreciate;
- management time is unduly spent in arguments with business units over charges for services, even though market rates may have been impartially checked (say, by the internal audit department);
- additional administrative costs may be excessive.

The decision as to whether to operate treasury as a profit centre may well depend on the particular 'style' of the company and the extent of centralization or decentralization of its activities.

## *SUMMARY*

In this chapter we have discussed the three main groups into which financial management decisions can be classified, namely investment, financing and dividends. We have identified the objectives of treasury management as being:

- acquiring the optimum finance for the business to meet its financial objectives;

- management of interest and exchange rate risks;
- providing advice to management on capital structure and dividend policy issues;
- management of the organization's liquid assets;
- liaison with the organization's banks.

In the remaining chapters we consider the activities of treasury management to see how the treasury manager may achieve the above objectives.

# 2

# Sources of Finance 1

Identifying optimal sources of finance for the organization is one of the key objectives for the treasury manager. In this chapter we identify the main sources of long-term finance available to companies, which broadly fall under the headings of share capital and loan finance. We also consider instruments such as options and warrants, which are sometimes issued as a means of raising finance. This chapter also deals with some of the basic terminology and practice of the stock market, and considers raising finance on the euromarkets.

## SHARE CAPITAL

### Equity shares

An equity interest in a company can be said to represent a share of the company's assets and a share of any profits earnt on those assets after other claims have been met. The equity shareholders are the owners of the business – they purchase shares (commonly called ordinary shares), the money is used by the company to buy assets, the assets are used to earn profits, and the assets and profits belong to the ordinary shareholders. Equity shares entail no agreement on the company's part to return to the shareholders the amount of their investment. Equity shares are sometimes referred to as the risk capital of a business: it is the equity shareholders that take most of the risk in business. Equity shares normally refers to ordinary shares.

### *Preference shares*

Preference shares entitle their holder to a fixed rate of dividend from the company each year. This dividend ranks for payment before other equity returns, and so the ordinary shareholders receive no dividend until the preference shareholders have been paid their fixed percentage. Preference shares carry part-ownership of the company and allow due participation in the profits of the business. In fact, their dividend is an appropriation of profits, so if a bad year means no profits, it means no dividend for the preference shareholders.

This point constitutes the essential distinction between preference shares and debentures. Debenture-holders are not part-owners of the company; their interest claims have to be met whether the company has made a profit or not. Interest payments are not an appropriation of profits. It is for this reason that the tax treatment of each of the two forms of fixed-percentage capital is different. Debenture interest, as a charge, is a tax-deductible expense, and like any other form of tax-allowable expenditure it reduces the company's tax bill. Preference dividends, as an appropriation of profits, are not tax-deductible. Tax is payable on the profits figure before the preference dividends are deducted. Consequently, a company earning profits and committed to paying out, say, 8 per cent on capital raised, would prefer to be paying it on debentures (for which the interest charge is net of tax) than on preference shares for which the company would have to stand the gross cost. Preference shares are thus a hybrid between equity and debt.

## *RAISING EQUITY CAPITAL – THE STOCK MARKET*

The stock market is a key feature of English-speaking economies – and seems to be set to grow elsewhere, as communism is replaced by capitalism, and even Western European economies are privatizing formerly public sector enterprises.

Its activities are mainly concerned with the secondary market, ie enabling investors to buy and sell shares in particular companies, without the companies themselves being directly affected. This is a vital role in the sense that, without the prospect of being able to sell shares when they wished, investors would be far less willing to buy them in the first place. Investors may buy and sell shares, hoping to make a capital gain as the share price rises. The capital gain will be realized when the share is sold to another investor at a price higher than that originally paid. Shares may be traded in one of two markets, according to the size and status of the company concerned. The largest companies will be traded on the Stock Exchange. The financial and other criteria necessary for a company to receive a full Stock Exchange quotation (or listing) are stringent. Companies which do not satisfy these criteria may be traded through the Alternative Investment Market (AIM), where entry conditions are significantly easier. Although AIM companies face similar regulations to fully listed companies, the entry procedures and ongoing obligations are much less onerous. In particular, there are no criteria concerning the capitalization of the company or its trading history.

Investors may speculate by buying shares in a particular company or sector of the market, believing that the value of those shares will rise shortly. Such a speculator is known as a 'bull'. Conversely, a 'bear' speculator is one who sells shares in the belief that their value is about to fall. If the company were to fail altogether, the shares would be worthless, but shareholders would not normally be required to use their own money to pay off the company's debts. Liability is said to be limited to the original investment. Creditors of the company need to be aware of this when trading or lending to the company, hence the need to include plc or Ltd in the company name.

Companies may become publicly quoted merely by making shares available by way of an *introduction*, ie existing shareholders being willing to sell some at a price. Otherwise, additional funds may be raised (ie for the company as well as existing shareholders) by means of new issues.

## New issues

Shares which come into circulation for the first time are called new issues. This section briefly outlines the ways in which this happens.

### Offer for sale

These offers may be of completely new shares or they may derive from the transfer to the public of shares already held privately. An issuing house, normally a merchant bank, acquires the shares and then offers them to the public at a fixed price. The offers are usually made in the form of a prospectus detailed in the *Financial Times* and other newspapers, sometimes in an abbreviated form. Buying new issues through the prospectus in the newspaper avoids dealing charges.

Other examples of such issues include government privatizations; *and* privately held shares transferred to the public. It is easier for prospective purchasers to form a judgement about such companies where there is some track record, rather than with offers for a completely new company such as Eurotunnel.

Some investors apply for new issues in the hope of selling immediately and reaping a quick profit. For this to succeed the number of shares purchased must be sufficiently high to cover selling charges. For oversubscribed issues, the allocation may be scaled down, in which case the applicant may receive only a small number of shares. The strategy of selling immediately is called stagging (and investors who do it are called stags). There have been some notable successes for stags, particularly in some of the privatization issues, but there have also been cases of where the initial dealing price has been substantially below the offer price. The most notable example of the latter was the offer for sale of BP shares in 1987.

### Offer for sale by tender

This method of issue is similar to that above, the only difference being that the shares are not issued at a fixed price. Subscribers must tender for the shares at, or above, a minimum fixed price. The shares are allotted at the highest price at which they will all be taken up. This is known as the strike price.

## Prospectus issue

In a prospectus issue, or public issue, a company offers its shares direct to the general public. An issuing house may act as an agent, but this type of issue will not be underwritten which makes this type of issue risky, and also very rare.

## Placing

In this type of issue the shares are not offered to the public, but the issuing house will arrange for the shares to be issued to its institutional clients. This method has become the most popular method of issue in the UK, being cheaper and quicker to arrange than most other methods.

## Rights issues

In a rights issue, the company sets out to raise additional funds from its existing shareholders. It does this by giving them the opportunity to purchase additional shares. These shares are normally offered at a price lower than the current share price quoted, otherwise shareholders will not be prepared to buy, since they could have purchased more shares at the existing price anyway. The company cannot offer an unlimited supply at this lower price, otherwise the market price would fall to this value. Accordingly, the offer they make to the existing shareholders is limited. For example, they may offer one new share for every four held.

Assuming this rights issue is taken up by the existing shareholders, the market price of the shares will readjust to a value above that of the rights issue but below the original market price. All things being equal, the new value of the shareholders' investment should equal the original value plus the money paid for the shares in the rights issue. If a shareholder ignores the rights issue, the number of shares held will have remained the same but the value of each will have dropped. So ignoring the rights issue is not a recommended course of action. The normal thing to do in these circumstances is to sell all or part of the option to acquire new shares at the lower price. If the option on all the new shares is sold, then the result is some cash and a holding of less value than hitherto. In theory the cash should compensate for the loss in value of the holding. It is possible to sell only part of the option and to use the money received to purchase the unsold part. In this way the value of the original holding can be maintained. Dealing charges will be payable to a stockbroker or bank for doing this.

Say, for example, a company's shares are trading at 400p each, and the directors announce a 1 for 4 rights issue at 300p. Other things being equal, after the issue, the company's shares can be expected to fall to $(4 \times 400p + 1 \times 300p) \div 5 = 380p$. This means that the right to buy 1 new share at 300p is worth $380p - 300p$, ie 80p; this will determine the value of the rights in the market place. The company will sell any rights not taken up, and compensate the shareholder accordingly.

If the company had 100 million old shares in existence, it will raise £75 million by way of the rights issue. Clearly, it does not really matter whether this is called 25 million at 300p, 50 million at 150p or any other feasible combination. The directors' freedom will be restricted by the number of authorized but unissued shares in existence, and the nominal value of the shares, but even these are variable in the long run. Merchant bankers normally advise only a small 'discount' from the prevailing price, but that may simply be to make their underwriting business look justified. The real question is whether the £75 million will be invested wisely, but this tends to be squeezed out by futile debate as to what the price should be.

### *Share splits and bonus issues*

These are shares issued without payment to holders of existing ordinary shares. They are issued because the price of the existing shares has become unwieldy. Bonus issues are at the initiative of the company directors, with the subsequent approval of the share-holder. Obviously these additional shares are normally accepted by the shareholders, but they are not getting something for nothing even though they are called bonus shares. This is because, if all other things are unchanged, the value of the company remains unal-tered. Accordingly if, before the bonus issue, there were 1 million shares each valued at 220p, then if there was a one-for-one bonus issue resulting in the number of shares increasing to 2 million the price of the shares would fall to 110p. Thus the shareholders would have twice as many shares each with half the value. In many cases, bonus issues are made in different ratios to one new share to each existing share but the same principle that the value of the holding is unchanged remains. Consequently, selling the shares from the bonus issue reduces the value of the individual's holding. Usually bonus issues are of ordinary shares but the issue can be in the form of preference shares.

## Equity options

An option gives its buyer the right, but not the obligation, to buy or sell a specific quantity of shares at a specific price on or before a specified future date. It is not necessary to own the shares concerned in order to deal in the options.

In the UK there are two forms of equity options: *traditional* options, and *traded* options. Traditional options may be exercised only on a specified date, and the option cannot be sold on to anyone else. Traded options can be exercised throughout their life, and are freely tradable.

In the UK, the London International Financial Futures and Options Exchange (LIFFE) provides a market for traded options on individual equity shares and on the FTSE 100 Index. Equity and index options allow investors the opportunity to take advan-tage of individual share price movements and movements in the market as a whole, and to profit when the market is falling as well as rising.

There are two types of option. A *call* option gives the holder the right, but not the obligation, to buy shares at a fixed price. A *put* option gives the holder the right, but not the obligation, to sell shares at a fixed price.

Traded options on individual equity shares may be dealt only in whole contracts, and each contract normally represents an option on 1,000 shares of the underlying security. They have a maximum life of nine months, with expiry dates set on a quarterly cycle.

Options have a number of uses:

- as insurance, to protect an existing shareholding from a fall in the share price over a specific time period;
- to speculate on the price of a share, or on the market as a whole;
- to make an upfront payment to buy (or receive an advance from selling) a share at a price fixed in advance;
- to generate additional income from a shareholding by selling call options in the hope that the option will not be exercised.

Table 2.1 shows how traded option price information is displayed in some newspapers, using data for an imaginary company Molier plc. The market price of the underlying security is 657p. LIFFE ensures that options are available with *exercise prices* above and below the current market price, and in this case options are available with exercise prices of 650p and 700p. The exercise price is the price at which an option gives the holder the right to buy or sell the underlying shares. Options on Molier plc shares are available with expiry dates in January, April and July. Once the January options expire, they will be replaced with options having October expiry dates.

A premium is paid at the time an option is purchased. The premium for the January 650 call is 20p. This implies that for 20p, an investor could buy the right to buy a Molier plc share before the January expiry date for a price of 650p.

An investor buying a call option is anticipating a rise in the price of the underlying security before the option expiry date. The

**Table 2.1** Traded options price information

| Option | | Calls | | | Puts | | |
|---|---|---|---|---|---|---|---|
| | | January | April | July | January | April | July |
| Molier plc | 650 | 20 | 42 | 50 | 11 | 26 | 40 |
| (657*) | 700 | 3 | 20 | 28 | 46 | 55 | 70 |

*Note*: *Underlying security price

investor could profit from such a rise either by purchasing the underlying share or by purchasing a call option. Purchasing 1,000 shares in Molier plc would cost £6,570. Buying one January 650 call contract would cost £200.

The price of the option will fluctuate depending on supply and demand, but will also be determined by the relationship between the exercise price and the price of the underlying shares. If the share price increases to, say, 668p before the middle of January, the January 650 call option would also have risen in value to, say, 28p. The option contract would now be worth £280. The option has increased in value by 40 per cent compared with a 2.7 per cent increase in the underlying share price.

To realize the profit, the option could be closed out by selling the option back to the market. Notice that exercising the option in this case would result in a purchase price for the underlying share of 670p (exercise price 650p + option premium 20p), compared with a current market price of 668p, and thus would not be worth while. This demonstrates the advantage of being able to trade the option itself, closing out being far more likely in practice than exercising the option.

If the share price does not increase before expiry date, or if it falls, the maximum loss that the investor will incur is the option premium of 20p. This loss could be reduced by selling the option back to the market before the value of the option falls to zero.

# *DEBT FINANCE*

## *Debentures*

A debenture is a document issued by a company containing an acknowledgement of indebtedness. It need not give, although it usually does, a charge on the assets of the company. The Companies Acts define 'debenture' as including debenture stock and bonds. It is quite common for the expressions debenture and bond to be used interchangeably. Company debentures can also be referred to as 'loan stock'.

Usually a debenture is a bond given in exchange for money lent to the company. Debentures can be offered to the public only if the application form is accompanied by a prospectus.

The company agrees to repay the principal to the lender by some future date, and in each year up to repayment it will pay a stated rate of interest in return for the use of the funds. The debenture-holder is a creditor of the company, and the interest has to be paid each year before a dividend is paid to any class of shareholder.

### *Secured or unsecured*

Debentures and debenture stock can be secured or unsecured. It is usual, however, to use the expression 'debenture' when referring to the more secure form of issue, and 'loan stock' for less secure issues. When secured, this is by means of a trust deed. The deed usually charges in favour of the trustees the whole or part of the property of the company. The advantages of a trust deed are that a prior charge cannot be obtained on the property without the consent of the debenture-holders, the events on which the principal is to be repaid are specified, and power given for the trustees to appoint a receiver and in certain events to carry on the business and enforce contracts.

The debentures can be secured by a charge upon the whole or a specific part of a company's assets, or they can be secured by a floating charge upon the assets of the company. In this latter case the company is not precluded from selling its assets. The latter case is known as a general lien, whereas the debenture issued on the security of a specific asset is a mortgage debenture or mortgage bond. With a floating charge, when the company makes a default in observing the terms of the debentures, a receiver may be appointed and the charge becomes fixed, with the power to deal in the assets passing into the hands of the receiver. Such restrictions are referred to as 'covenants'.

### Convertibles

Convertibles are hybrids between equity capital and debt finance. They offer investors a fixed return, but also give the investor the right to convert into the underlying ordinary shares of the company at fixed terms. There are various types of convertible: convertible debentures, convertible loan stock and convertible preference shares.

All carry the right to convert into the underlying ordinary shares, and represent less risk to the investor than the ordinary shares because they have greater priority for repayment should the company be liquidated. The most secure is the convertible debenture which is secured upon the tangible assets of the company.

One advantage which is often quoted for convertible debt is that it is cheaper than ordinary debt finance since the conversion option allows the security to be issued with a lower coupon rate than would otherwise be the case. Although it is true that the coupon on convertibles is lower, this does not mean that the overall cost is lower since the expected cost of the conversion option must also be considered.

The lower coupon rate of a convertible may, however, be advantageous from a liquidity point of view. This form of finance may suit a project where the cash inflows are expected to be low in the early years.

Prior to conversion, the security will represent debt finance and will, therefore, increase the level of gearing of a company. Convertibles are seen as a way of issuing deferred equity. This may be particularly advantageous if existing shareholders want to minimize any loss of control since the number of shares issued via a convertible (assuming conversion takes place) will be smaller than if straight equity were issued.

A useful aspect of convertibles is that, assuming the company's share price rises sufficiently to force conversion, the debt is self-liquidating. Since it is replaced by equity, conversion will reduce the level of gearing and thereby enable the company to issue further debt finance.

While convertibles remain as debt, the interest is tax-deductible. this gives rise to the tax advantage which also accompanies other forms of debt finance. However, since the coupon rate on this security is lower than that associated with normal debt, the tax advantage is consequently reduced also.

As the convertible stock carries the right of conversion into the underlying ordinary shares, its price will be directly linked to that of the equity for as long as the conversion option exists. As the ordinary shares increase in price, so will the convertible, and vice versa. The relationship between the price of the ordinary share and the convertible is usually expressed in one of two ways as illustrated below.

*Illustrative example*

Oldham plc has in issue convertible loan stock with a coupon rate of 10 per cent. Each £100 nominal is convertible into 20 ordinary shares. The market price of the convertible is £108, while the current ordinary share price is 480p.

Calculate (1) the conversion premium; and (2) the conversion value.

*Solution*

The conversion terms are: £100 loan stock = 20 ordinary shares. This is known as the *conversion ratio*.

The conversion terms could also be expressed as: £5 loan stock = 1 ordinary share.

1. The *conversion premium* measures how much more expensive it is to buy the convertible loan stock than the underlying ordinary share.

The cost of buying £5 loan stock is:

$$£5 \times \frac{108}{100} = £5.40$$

compared with the cost of buying 1 ordinary share, £4.80.

The conversion premium is therefore:

$$\frac{5.40 - 4.80}{4.80} = 12.5\%$$

In this case, it is more expensive to purchase the loan stock and convert than to purchase one ordinary share directly.

2. The *conversion value* is calculated as the market value of ordinary shares (MPS) that is equivalent to one unit of the convertible.

$$\text{Conversion value} = \text{conversion ratio} \times \text{MPS}$$
$$\text{(ordinary shares)}$$
$$= 20 \times £4.80$$
$$= £96$$

Note that from this calculation of conversion value, the conversion premium may also be stated as:

$$\frac{£108 - £96}{£96} = 12.5\%.$$

## Warrants

Warrants are options to buy shares in the company at a given price within a given period. They can be traded on the market and are sometimes issued with loan stock as a 'sweetener'.

Share warrants issued in conjunction with a debt security will put the holder in an overall position which is very similar to that of a convertible-holder. Thus it follows that the holder has both debt and equity interest in the issuing firm. However, it may be argued that investors will find warrants more attractive than a convertible since they can sell warrants separately, whereas the conversion option is an integral part of convertible securities.

The warrant, like the conversion option, will enable the coupon rate to be reduced on the debt instrument. The amount of this reduction will depend upon the value of the warrant.

Unlike a convertible, the debt issued with warrants will run to maturity thus maintaining the tax deduction. The warrants, if exercised, will also result in new capital being raised; this may be useful if expansion of the project which was originally undertaken is being contemplated. However, the timing of the exercising of warrants is determined by investors and may not result in extra capital when needed by the company.

Debt issued with warrants is not self-liquidating and, therefore, additional finance will be needed for redemption. The use of both convertibles and warrants represents an attempt to make debt capital more attractive to investors; they also have characteristics which may make them useful to a company as part of its financing.

### *The euromarkets*

The 'euro' term is a catch-all tag used to refer to an investment in a currency held outside its country of origin. It does not suggest that the investment is in Europe, or that the currency is European. For example, US dollars deposited in a Japanese bank would be referred to as eurodollars.

The increase in international trade has meant that significant amounts of currencies such as US dollars, Japanese yen and UK sterling are held on deposit outside their home countries. These deposits are then loaned out by the banks. *Eurocurrencies* are effectively 'stateless' money, so any transactions are not subject to the domestic rules and regulations of any financial centre. London has become the main centre for eurocurrency transactions, although the eurocurrency market is not a domestic UK market and most eurocurrency transactions are carried out by overseas banks based there.

Eurocurrencies can be deposited or borrowed for relatively short periods – typically three months – or for a number of years. The *syndicated loan market* developed from the short-term eurocurrency market. A syndicate of banks is brought together by a lead bank to provide medium- to long-term currency loans to large multinational companies. These loans may run to the equivalent of hundreds of millions of pounds. By arranging a syndicate of banks to provide the loan, the lead bank reduces its risk exposure.

*Eurobonds* are bonds issued in a currency outside its country of origin. Large companies, banks and some governments raise money through issuing bonds in the eurobond market, in a similar way that companies and governments issue bonds in their domestic markets. The main difference is that borrowers are tapping the 'euro' pool of stateless money. This means that the eurobond market is not totally accountable to any particular government, which leads to fewer controls or regulation.

Eurobonds are usually issued in bearer rather than registered form, which means that the bondholder does not have to declare identification. Possession of the bond is sufficient to prove ownership. Interest is paid gross, allowing investors to pay their own domestic tax, although the eurobond market has been criticized as being a haven for tax-shy investors.

## SUMMARY

In this first chapter on sources of finance we have identified the main long-term sources available to a company. Reliance on equity capital as the main form of long-term finance is a distinguishing feature of the UK and US economies. The value of a company to its equity shareholders is a function of projected cash flows to them (dividends less rights issues).

We investigate other potential sources of finance in Chapters 3 and 5, while in Chapter 4 we investigate the implications for a company of combining debt and equity in the capital structure.

# 3

# Sources of Finance 2

In this chapter we consider medium-term sources of finance, in the form of term loans and leasing agreements. We also consider the specific problems of fund raising for small businesses, and identify some sources that are particularly appropriate for small businesses.

## *TERM LOANS*

Term loans are offered by the high street banks, and their popularity has increased for a number of reasons, not least their accessibility. A term loan is for a fixed amount with a fixed repayment schedule. Usually the interest rate applied is slightly less than for a bank overdraft. The lender will require security to cover the amount borrowed, and an arrangement fee is payable dependent on the amount borrowed. Term loans also have the following qualities:

- *They are negotiated easily and quickly* This is particularly important when a cash-flow problem has not been identified until recently, and a quick but significant fix is needed.
- *Banks may offer flexible repayments* High street banks will often devise new lending methods to suit their customers; eg no capital repayments for, say, two years, thus avoiding unnecessary overborrowing to fund capital repayment.
- *Variable interest rates* This may be important given the uncertainty that exists with interest rates.

Most medium-term finance is used by small businesses, as a result of the problems they face in raising capital.

## LEASING

A business may buy equipment outright, or on hire purchase or lease it. An evaluation of the lease-or-buy decision will usually require an understanding of the basics of taxation. You may be asked, for example, to compare the cash-flow consequences of buying/leasing some equipment. Among the points to remember are that the buying route leads you into the 'reducing balance' arithmetic of capital allowances, and raises the question of the capacity of the business to use all the allowances to which it is entitled.

The distinguishing feature of a lease is that one party (the lessee) obtains the use of an asset for a period of time, whereas the legal ownership of the asset remains with the other party (the lessor). The leasing agreement does not give the lessee the right to final ownership.

Leasing is common for aircraft, vehicles, plant and machinery, computers and other office equipment. More recently, it has been touted as a means of bringing private finance into public sector projects, eg transport and healthcare sectors. Total business in the UK is around £12 billion per annum. The industry has had its share of adverse publicity in recent years, including:

- Cases of misrepresentation in the photocopier segment. The leading trade body, the Finance and Leasing Association, is seeking to improve matters through issuing guidelines as to clarity in contracts, and the response to complaints.
- Some spectacular collapses and severe financial difficulties for some lessors. In some cases, 'aggressive income recognition' (taking all the profit on the deal at the outset, even where there is an agreement to take the asset back at the lessee's request) has hidden the problems from public view for long periods of time.

Properly structured and controlled, however, it can be a valuable and flexible form of finance. Although they like to stress their differences from the mainstream banks, most general leasing companies are actually subsidiaries of banks. They have the strength of the banks behind them, therefore, but are able to focus on the very special situations for which leasing is appropriate, and would claim to be far more flexible than their parents. The justification for leasing, however, relies heavily on two distortions in the capital market: taxation and accounting.

The UK tax system – because it is based on a version of accounting profits rather than cash flows – has an adverse effect on investment. If for any reason the enterprise is not paying mainstream tax (including local authorities and other 'not-for-profit' organizations, for example), it will not be able to utilize the capital allowances – making the net present value even more negative. Leasing enables another company with tax capacity to buy the asset, claim the capital allowances, and pass on at least part of the benefit to the user in the form of a lower financing charge than would otherwise be the case. On a smaller scale, where the lessee's effective tax rate is lower than the lessor's (eg small company rate of 21 per cent versus standard rate of 31 per cent), a benefit can be created and shared.

The restrictions which are placed on directors' freedom of manoeuvre – in Articles of Association, banking covenants and Stock Exchange agreements – are expressed in terms of accounting numbers. Total borrowings, for example, are usually limited to a defined percentage of the net worth (equity capital) of the enterprise. Where these limits have been reached, or are forecast to be reached, and the company cannot or does not wish to increase its permanent capital, there is obviously something to be said for an arrangement which enables it to have the use of an asset which does not have to appear in its accounts.

### Who bears the risk?

Two kinds of lease can be identified: finance leases and operating leases. A finance lease is an agreement whereby the user of the asset, the lessee, obtains the use of the asset for the whole, or substantially the whole, of the asset's useful life. The Accounting Standard for lease agreements (SSAP 21) states that a finance lease may be presumed if the present value of the minimum lease payments amounts to 90 per cent or more of the present value of the asset's fair value. The accounting treatment required reflects the 'substance over form' approach adopted by the Standard. Lease finance is sold as being:

- stable – in the sense that, once negotiated, it will remain in place, not be subject to cancellation like an overdraft facility; the risk associated with the residual value of the asset can be transferred to the lessor;
- fixed price or suitably hedged;
- smooth, in terms of its effect on cash flow (as compared with outright purchase);
- cheap – thanks to greater security for the lender, ie the legal ownership of the asset (though some depreciate very quickly, or would be difficult to reuse);
- tailored to individual needs, and flexible, eg inclusive of a facility to upgrade;
- inclusive of some services, eg buying and selling, registration and other administration, maintenance and disaster recovery.

There are some drawbacks, of course, including the possibility that some government grants might be missed. The economic effect of leasing stems from the fact that it is the owner (who is not necessarily the user) of the asset who is entitled to the allowances. They may be worth more, say, to a bank which has high profits and low capital expenditure than to a manufacturer with a big capital expenditure programme relative to its taxable profits. The practice was very popular, for example, in the days of high inflation, price control, 100 per cent first-year allowances and stock relief.

In some situations, therefore, the interest built into the leasing arrangement, being in effect after-tax, can be lower than that which would be incurred by users had they borrowed money in the usual way (eg if the company is not making a taxable profit, and is not able to use the tax allowance).

## Finance leases

Finance leases are essentially term loans. These have to be shown in the lessee's accounts as assets and liabilities, and the depreciation and financing charged against profits.

The term of the lease normally extends over the full useful life of the asset. The lessor, therefore, receives lease payments which will fully cover the cost of the asset. The agreement will usually not be cancellable and will not provide for any maintenance of the asset. The leasing company is not normally involved in dealing with the assets themselves, being a bank or finance company. The asset is selected by the firm which will use it, which negotiates price, delivery, etc. The leasing company simply buys the asset and arranges a lease contract with the lessee. At the end of the lease period there will usually be an agreement where the sale proceeds from the asset are shared between the lessor and lessee, or if the lessee desires it can carry on using the asset for payment of a nominal amount each year, called a *peppercorn rent*.

## Sale and leaseback

Companies can use what is known as a sale and leaseback arrangement in order to convert certain assets which the company owns into funds, and yet for the company to still continue to use the assets. For example, if a building is sold to an insurance company or some other financial intermediary and then leased back from the purchaser, the company has secured an immediate cash inflow. The only cash outflow is the rental payments that it now has to make. These rental payments are allowed as a tax-deductible expense. However, the company may be subject to capital gains tax, which will arise if the sale price is in excess of the written-down value as agreed by the tax authorities.

It must be remembered, however, that the leased asset no longer belongs to the company; the lease may one day come to an end and then alternative assets will have to be obtained.

This financing possibility is particularly applicable to assets which appreciate in value, such as land, buildings or some other form of property. It is particularly appropriate to companies owning the properties freehold, and to institutions such as insurance companies or pension funds which are interested in holding long-term secure assets. The property is leased back at a negotiated annual rental, although with long leasebacks there will need to be a provision for the revision of the rental at certain intervals of time.

Clearly, the sale and leaseback releases funds which can be used for some other investment. In the 1950s a number of takeovers were financed by this means. Assets were sold and leased back; the cash obtained from the sale was used to finance the purchase of another company. If the acquired company had substantial property so much the better, for this property could then be sold to an insurance company and leased back.

## Operating leases

Operating leases are treated very much like contract hire. They do not appear on the lessee's balance sheet, and the fee for the hire is charged directly against profits.

These agreements will usually not last for the full life of an asset. They are offered by companies who manufacture or deal in the particular product, often incorporating maintenance and other services. The lease can be cancelled and the equipment returned. Operating leases are common for office and business equipment, eg photocopiers, computers and motor vehicles. Lessors will not recover their full investment on any one lease but will hope to lease a particular asset several times over its life. Operating leases are particularly useful for industries where there is a rapid change in technology which makes it necessary to have the latest equipment, eg computers.

# *LEASE-OR-BUY DECISIONS*

The decision to lease or buy an asset is a financing decision which will be made only once the decision to invest in the asset has been taken. The decision to invest in the asset would be determined by discounting the operational costs and benefits from using the asset at the cost of capital normally used by the enterprise to evaluate projects, typically its weighted average cost of capital. Investing in the asset would be justified if a positive net present value (NPV) is obtained.

The financing decision is then concerned with identifying the least-cost financing option. In evaluating the financing decision, it is usually assumed that the enterprise would have to borrow funds in order to purchase the asset.

## *Example*

Pleasure-boat operators Woodfield and Hills Ltd are considering investing in a new boat for their fleet. The company can either borrow the necessary funds from its bank at 9 per cent and purchase the boat, or enter into a finance lease involving five annual year-end payments of £24,000. The new boat costs £100,000 and would attract capital allowances at 25 per cent on a reducing balance over its five-year life for its owners. Corporation tax is 33 per cent, payable in the year of the relevant profits. Calculate which of the two options, borrowing or leasing, is financially more advantageous for Woodfield and Hills Ltd.

## *Solution*

### 1. Borrow and purchase

The first stage is to calculate the capital allowances attracted by the purchase of the boat as shown in Table 3.1. The first capital allowance is assumed to be claimed at the end of year 1.

**Table 3.1** Capital allowance calculation

| Year | Working | Allowance | Tax shield (33%) |
|------|---------|-----------|------------------|
| 1 | £100,000 × 25% | 25,000 | 8,250 |
| 2 | (£100,000 – £25,000) × 25% | 18,750 | 6,188 |
| 3 | (£75,000 – £18,750) × 25% | 14,063 | 4,641 |
| 4 | (£56,250 – £14,063) × 25% | 10,547 | 3,481 |
|   |   | 68,360 |   |
| 5 | Balance (£100,000 – £68,360) | 31,640 | 10,441 |
|   |   | 100,000 |   |

The after-tax cash flows associated with this financing option should be discounted at the after-tax cost of borrowing, which is $9\% \times (1 - 0.33) = 6\%$. This is illustrated in Table 3.2.

**Table 3.2** Appraisal of borrow and purchase

| Year | Investment £ | Tax shield £ | Discount factor @ 6% | Present value £ |
|------|--------------|--------------|----------------------|-----------------|
| 0 | (100,000) |  | 1.000 | (100,000) |
| 1 |  | 8,250 | 0.943 | 7,780 |
| 2 |  | 6,188 | 0.890 | 5,507 |
| 3 |  | 4,641 | 0.840 | 3,898 |
| 4 |  | 3,481 | 0.792 | 2,757 |
| 5 |  | 10,441 | 0.747 | 7,799 |
|   |   |   |   | (72,259) |

Note that the interest charges from borrowing are reflected in the discount rate used.

## 2. Finance lease

Under current UK legislation depreciation on leased assets is treated as a tax-deductible expense, as is the interest element of

**Table 3.3** Appraisal of finance lease

| Year | Lease payment £ | Tax shield 33% £ | Net cash £ | Discount factor @ 6% | Present value £ |
|---|---|---|---|---|---|
| 1 | (24,000) | 7,920 | (16,080) | 0.943 | (15,163) |
| 2 | (24,000) | 7,920 | (16,080) | 0.890 | (14,311) |
| 3 | (24,000) | 7,920 | (16,080) | 0.840 | (13,507) |
| 4 | (24,000) | 7,920 | (16,080) | 0.792 | (12,735) |
| 5 | (24,000) | 7,920 | (16,080) | 0.747 | (12,012) |
| | | | | | (67,728) |

the finance lease payments. However, for illustration purposes, we shall assume that it is the full finance lease payment that is allowable for tax.

The after-tax cash flows associated with this financing option should again be discounted at the after-tax cost of borrowing on the basis that the minimum return necessary to accept the lease contract will be the after-tax return obtainable on a similar loan. This is illustrated in Table 3.3.

In this example, the finance lease is financially the most advantageous method of financing the investment in the boat.

## Selecting the discount rate

An issue in this kind of evaluation is the discount rate to use: the *cost of capital* to the entity (which has presumably been used to evaluate the decision to acquire the plant) or the cost of the *next best alternative means of finance* (eg an overdraft). The discount rate that should be used in all investment decisions is the opportunity cost. If we argue that leasing is a direct substitute for borrowing, the opportunity cost of leasing is the cost of borrowing.

There can be a complication when, say, £100-worth of leasing is not replacing £100-worth of borrowing. It could be that the debt capacity of the kind of equipment being leased is different from that of the existing assets of the company. The leased equipment could then either increase or decrease the gearing possibilities of the lessee. If £100 of lease liability is a substitute for less than £100 of debt, then a cost of capital other than the borrowing rate will have to be used.

## *Repayment of borrowings*

Under the borrow and purchase option in the above example, no consideration was given as to how or when the borrowings were to be repaid. This simplifies the arithmetic required to calculate the present value of this financing option.

Let us now consider the workings required if the borrowings of £100,000 were to be repaid to the bank in equal annual year-end instalments comprising principal and interest at 9 per cent per annum.

### *Solution*

The first stage is to identify the amount of the equal annual instalments required to service the bank loan.

Dividing the amount of the loan by the annuity factor for five years at 9 per cent:

$$\frac{£100,000}{3.890} = £25,707$$

Each instalment then needs to be split down between the repayment of principal and interest on an actuarial basis as shown in Table 3.4.

When discounting the cash flows associated with the borrow and purchase option at the after-tax cost of borrowing, it should be remembered that the annual instalment includes the interest payments on the loan and so the tax shield relating to the interest must be included as a cash flow as shown in Table 3.5. Allowing for rounding differences, the present value obtained should be identical to our original answer for the borrow and purchase option in the previous section.

**Table 3.4** Actuarial table to apportion interest

| Year | Balance b/f | Interest @ 9% | Annual instalment | Balance c/f |
|------|-------------|---------------|-------------------|-------------|
| | £ | £ | £ | £ |
| 1 | 100,000 | 9,000 | (25,707) | 83,293 |
| 2 | 83,293 | 7,496 | (25,707) | 65,082 |
| 3 | 65,082 | 5,857 | (25,707) | 45,232 |
| 4 | 45,232 | 4,071 | (25,707) | 23,596 |
| 5 | 23,596 | 2,111* | (25,707) | |

*Note*: * Rounding difference.

**Table 3.5** Appraisal of borrow and purchase

| Year | Annual instalment | Tax shield on interest | Tax shield on capital allowances | Net cash flow | Discount factor @ 6% | PV |
|------|-------------------|------------------------|----------------------------------|---------------|----------------------|-----|
| | £ | £ | £ | £ | | £ |
| 1 | (25,707) | 2,970 | 8,250 | (14,487) | 0.943 | (13,661) |
| 2 | (25,707) | 2,474 | 6,188 | (17,045) | 0.890 | (15,170) |
| 3 | (25,707) | 1,933 | 4,641 | (19,133) | 0.840 | (16,072) |
| 4 | (25,707) | 1,343 | 3,481 | (20,883) | 0.792 | (16,539) |
| 5 | (25,707) | 697 | 10,441 | (14,569) | 0.747 | (10,883) |
| | | | | | | (72,325) |

## Lessee and lessor

In the example above we had only to consider the position of the lessee and whether they should lease or buy. We could also look at the arrangement from the perspective of the lessor.

If lessors and lessees can both claim the same capital allowances, both have the same cost of capital. If the leasing company does not add on a profit percentage, or if the cost of capital to the lessees plus the add-on percentage is the same as the cost of capital to the lessors, then the lessees will be indifferent whether they lease or buy. Leasing can be attractive to lessees when they are faced with cash flows different from those of the lessors. Lessors will receive capital allowances if purchasing the asset, and will receive the lease payments as income.

### Example

Using the information from the Woodfield and Hills Ltd example above, evaluate the finance lease from the point of view of the lessor, assuming the lessor's required rate of return is 15 per cent after tax as shown in Table 3.6.

**Table 3.6** Lessor's evaluation of finance lease

| Year | Investment £ | Tax shield £ | Lease £ | Tax £ | Net cash flow £ | 15% DF | PV £ |
|---|---|---|---|---|---|---|---|
| 0 | (100,000) | | | | (100,000) | 1.000 | (100,000) |
| 1 | | 8,250 | 24,000 | (7,920) | 24,330 | 0.870 | 21,167 |
| 2 | | 6,188 | 24,000 | (7,920) | 22,268 | 0.756 | 16,835 |
| 3 | | 4,641 | 24,000 | (7,920) | 20,721 | 0.658 | 13,634 |
| 4 | | 3,481 | 24,000 | (7,920) | 19,561 | 0.572 | 11,189 |
| 5 | | 10,441 | 24,000 | (7,920) | 26,521 | 0.497 | 13,181 |
| | | | | | | | (23,994) |

### Solution

Perhaps, not surprisingly, the leasing company could not justify repayments of £24,000, as this leads to a negative NPV. The lessor will have to increase the lease rentals.

# FINANCING OF SMALL BUSINESSES

Individual enterprises come into being, they grow, they shrink, they cease to exist. Positive encouragement of small businesses is advocated in many quarters, as the natural offset to the decline of the very large corporations. Indeed, either voluntarily, or as a result of the attention of predators, some large companies have been subject to 'unbundling' or 'demerging'.

In the first unified budget (November 1993) the Chancellor expressed the view that in the UK 'we generate plenty of budding entrepreneurs and any number of inventions and good ideas. Yet all too often, those ideas stay on the drawing board as money is channelled instead into the safer, larger companies. In my opinion the biggest contribution any Chancellor can make to reducing unemployment over the medium term is to ensure that the conditions are in place for new businesses to become better established and small businesses to grow'. It is estimated that there are about 2.5 million small businesses in the UK.

Small businesses tend to be privately owned, of course, and part of the problem is that owners are anxious not to cede control to (or share equity rewards with) outsiders. This can have the effect of restricting the rate of growth to that which can be funded by retentions, but judicious subcontracting and the use of leasing, hire purchase, factoring, licensing etc, can mitigate this.

Owners of small businesses are especially critical of the high street banks, especially now that authority previously devolved to local managers has been centralized, and there has been a shift away from customers to products. Consequently, as one consultant remarked: 'When you ask your local bank manager for a loan, don't be surprised if he says he has to refer it to head office, but meanwhile tries to sell you some life assurance.'

Lending to small businesses used to be seen as an attractive part of any bank's portfolio. The rate of interest was good, and the client was likely to need other services on which the banks could make money. From time to time, however, attention is drawn to the difficulties small businesses have in obtaining the finance to support their growth strategies, at anything less than penal rates of interest (several percentage points higher than that at which large businesses can borrow) and the additional charges they face. Among the explanations given for this situation are that:

- the costs of monitoring such loans are high or even prohibitive, in which case the risk is greater, ie the investment has more of the characteristics of equity than lending;
- the banks themselves are involved in a competitive struggle for existence, and have gone through difficult times, incurring substantial bad debts during recessions and in the emergence from recessions, exacerbated recently by the unprecedented fall in the values of properties used as security;
- (consequently?) the regulators attach a higher risk weighting to corporate loans when assessing capital adequacy, with the result that banks are predisposed towards property and government loans;
- some of those other services are being provided by 'niche' players who are able to specialize and, therefore, offer better terms than the full-range banks.

As regards responses to this situation, the following trends are worth noting.

- The banking industry is itself in transition, with strategies based on consolidation and focus clearing the way for a stronger role to be played – possibly involving greater use of long-term loans. An enquiry mounted by the Bank of England reported, in January 1994, that banks were 'committed to the finance of the small firm sector, and were trying to provide alternatives to the traditional overdraft'.
- Some banks are even prepared to consider equity stakes, so as to share in the successes as well as the failures.
- Schemes involving more specific securitization of assets are being developed.
- Perhaps the most significant trend for financial managers: some banks are calling for more information to justify the original facility, and to monitor its use. The key information is likely to take the form of a cash-flow forecast. If this prompts them to place less emphasis on accounting statements, they will be more amenable at the time the small

company needs their help – ahead of an expansion which has an adverse effect on the short-term profit/asset profile of the business.

## *Venture capital*

Venture capital is the name given to equity finance provided to young, unquoted businesses to help them to expand. The traditional structure of a venture capital fund has been a 10-year partnership (of investors such as pension funds) but, in recent years, there have been moves to create more flexible forms, eg rolling one-year funds, a guarantee to return funds on request or, potentially, funds with unlimited life. There has also been a move towards a market in portfolios, with a view to offloading unsatisfactory performers, seeking economies of scale, etc.

The managers are rewarded by means of an annual fee (typically 2 per cent of the funds invested, but tending to taper off as funds get bigger) and part of the capital gain when the investments are realized. Though extremely significant in the 1980s, venture capital has been in decline in recent years, for a number of reasons:

- Investors have been disappointed with the results achieved so far, and are reluctant to commit further funds. The economic recession and the consequent difficulties for small businesses have been factors, but the level of management fees has also caused concern. The valuation of funds is not easy, which militates against reliable measurement of performance, assessment of potential and hence monitoring of the progress.
- Investee companies have been concerned at the short-termism displayed by the venture capitalists – in terms of requiring early reported profits (at the time of writing, with base rates well down into single figures, funds are telling prospective investees that they are looking for constant compound internal rates of return in excess of 30 per cent per annum (in the jargon of the industry, plums have to pay

for lemons) and an early exit (by way of flotation, a trade sale or refinancing on a more permanent basis).

The two problems interact, of course, with the moment of exit being the only time when a comprehensive measure of performance is possible. The funds tend to seek a definitive long-range plan, and rely on accounting numbers. Indeed, most funds are run by accountants and financiers (rather than experienced industrialists) and tend, therefore, to be risk averse. This may explain their apparent lack of interest in start-up finance schemes, which are relatively more time-consuming, higher risk and take longer to produce results. Rather, they have tended to concentrate on later-stage development and changes of ownership: management buy-outs, buy-ins and the hybrid 'bimbos' (involving both existing and new managers). Some tend to favour particular geographical areas, while others specialize in particular industries. Styles vary from hands on (most common where funds concentrate on particular industries or markets) through close monitoring to hands off.

Equity funds provide a basis for the company to raise further bank finance. Dividends can be delayed until the company is making profits.

### Business 'angels'

To judge from deals reported, venture capital funds are rarely interested in investing less than £250,000 on the grounds that monitoring progress is uneconomic. Below this level, companies may think in terms of business 'angels' (a term borrowed from show business), ie private individuals (eg big-company directors/managers who have retired with 'golden handshakes'), usually with time and expertise available as well as cash, and hence looking for a local, hands-on, involvement. They may come together in syndicates, led by an 'archangel'.

This practice is very big in the USA, where it is estimated to be three times as large a source of funds as the formal venture capital industry. There, lawyers and accountants tend to act as brokers. In the UK, it is a growing source, and the Government says it is keen to arrange introductions, via Training and Enterprise Councils and similar organizations, and to foster co-operation between small and large organizations.

Angels are more likely to be persuaded by outward- and forward-looking considerations, like strategic vision, intuition, flexibility and the identification of sources of competitive advantage, as well as the skills required to develop appropriate tactics and to manage operations. They would also look for the appropriate information systems, covering forecasting, decision support and monitoring. That first unified budget speech, mentioned earlier, introduced the Enterprise Initiative Scheme (EIS), as the successor to the Business Expansion Scheme, with effect from January 1994. The scheme enables a company to raise up to £1 million, in a form which is tax-efficient for the investor. Specifically:

- investors get tax relief (but restricted to the 20 per cent rate) on total investments of up to £150,000 per annum. The investment must be held for a minimum of five years, capital gains also being free (and capital losses may be set against income tax or capital gains tax);
- the investor can take an active interest, through a paid directorship, but financial involvement is limited to 30 per cent of the shares in issue;
- capital gains from elsewhere can be postponed to the extent that proceeds are invested in an EIS opportunity.

## *GOVERNMENT ASSISTANCE*

The UK government has introduced a number of schemes to help businesses, many of which are targeted at small- and medium-sized enterprises. *Regional Selective Assistance (RSA)* is aimed at giving discretionary grants to businesses that want to expand or relocate in an area that has been identified for special support. The grant is intended to help with projects that will create new jobs or protect existing ones. An example of this would be the *Regional Enterprise Grant (REG)* which is aimed at smaller businesses, whereby up to 15 per cent of the cost of a capital project (up to a maximum of £15,000) may be provided in the form of a grant.

Other support is aimed specifically to promote innovation and technology. These awards are not geographically targeted. Examples of these are: a *SMART Award*, which is worth up to £45,000 to support innovative technology in businesses with 50 employees or less; and the *Teaching Company Scheme (TCS)* which enables small businesses to employ a graduate for approximately 30 per cent of the market rate for up to two years.

The UK Government has recently announced the launch of a new Enterprise Fund aimed at supporting high-technology start-up companies. However, to finance this new fund, the Government has decided to axe its long-standing loan guarantee scheme.

## SUMMARY

In this chapter we have considered medium-term sources of finance, and looked specifically at sources of finance for small businesses. The medium-term sources reviewed were in the form of term loans and various forms of leasing agreement.

Small businesses often claim that it is difficult for them to raise capital at anything other than penal rates. This may reflect perceptions of risk, especially as regards the probability of repayment. The venture capital industry has not been as active as perhaps it should have been in financing small businesses, which may be why we have seen the emergence of business 'angels' and management buy-in teams.

# 4

# Capital Structure

A key element in the financing decision of an organization is to identify the cost of a source of finance, and to consider the overall cost of finance as reflected by the organization's capital structure. In this chapter we consider the cost of capital, and discuss a range of views as to the effect that capital structure has on the cost of capital.

## COST OF CAPITAL

We call the cut-off rate, which separates viable from non-viable opportunities, the cost of capital, and it is one of the fundamental disciplines of the capitalist market economy. Only those enterprises able to offer the prospect of a return in excess of the cost of capital will be able to attract the funds required to grow: those unable to do so will wither to extinction.

This discipline is translated into a criterion for the allocation of resources within enterprises. The higher the cost of capital, for instance, the lower will be the investment in equipment, in innovation, in training, and in working capital in anticipation of customers' needs, the higher will be the selling price which optimizes the return on a particular product, and so on.

### Cost of equity

Measuring the cost of equity is a very difficult task. The cost of equity must relate to the return which equity investors expect to reward them for the risk taken by investing in the company. However, this return is likely to vary from year to year.

Two common measures of the cost of equity capital are the dividend valuation model and the capital asset pricing model (CAPM). We begin with the basic form of the dividend valuation model as a method of calculating cost of equity.

$$r_e = \frac{d_1}{P_0}$$

where $r_e$ = cost of equity
$d_1$ = annual dividend
$P_0$ = market value of equity (ex dividend)

This basic model assumes a constant rate of dividends to perpetuity and ignores taxation. Assume £1 shares quoted at £2.50, dividend just paid of 20p, then

$$r_e = \frac{20}{250} = 0.08 \text{ or } 8\%$$

The model can be extended to incorporate growth in the dividends, $g$:

$$r_e = \frac{d_0(1 + g)}{P_0(\text{ex dividend})} + g$$

Assuming $g$ is constant at 5 per cent to perpetuity and the current dividend $d_0$ is 20p,

$$r_e = \frac{20(1.05)}{250} + 0.05 = 0.134, \text{ or } 13.4\%$$

The dividend valuation model as described above does not explicitly consider risk. Risk here is the risk that actual returns – ie dividends – will not be the same as expected returns. CAPM is a technique that enables risk to be incorporated into financial analysis.

Using CAPM to calculate the cost of equity:

$$r_e = r_f + [E(r_m) - r_f]\beta_j$$

where

$$\begin{aligned}
r_e &= \text{cost of equity} \\
r_f &= \text{risk-free rate of return} \\
E(r_m) &= \text{expected return from the market portfolio} \\
\beta_j &= \text{equity beta}
\end{aligned}$$

Assuming an equity beta of 1.4, an expected market return of 16 per cent and a risk-free rate of 10 per cent, then:

$$r_e = 10 + [16 - 10]\, 1.4 = 18.4\%$$

## Cost of debt

Thus far we have considered dividend valuation models relating to an ungeared company, so the next stage is to consider the effect of introducing debt into the calculation. Any fixed-interest debt, eg bonds or debentures, when issued will carry a *coupon rate*, ie the rate of interest payable on the *face or nominal value* of the debt. Thus, £100 (face value) of 7 per cent debentures has a *coupon rate* of 7 per cent.

When such debt is issued, the *coupon rate* will be fixed in accord with interest rates ruling in the market at that particular time for debt of similar nature and maturity. After issue of the debt, its *market value* will depend on the relationship of the *coupon rate* to the *rate of return required by investors* at any particular time. Thus, if the *market value* of £100 of 7 per cent debentures on a particular day is 90, then the *rate of return* required at that time (gross of tax) is $(7/90) \times 100 \approx 7.78\%$.

(a) Undated debt, eg undated debentures:

$$r_d = \frac{I(1 - t)}{MV\,(\text{ex interest})}$$

where

$r_d$ = cost of debt (after tax)
$I$ = annual interest
$t$ = rate of corporation tax (assumed immediately recoverable)
$MV$ = market value of debt (ex interest, ie immediately after payment)

Assume 7 per cent debentures quoted at 90 (ex interest), interest just paid, and corporation tax is 33 per cent, then:

$$r_d = \frac{7(0.67)}{90} \approx 0.052 \text{ or } 5.2\%$$

(b) Let us now expand the debt model to deal with forms of redeemable debt, eg redeemable debentures:

$r_d$ = discounting rate at which cash flows

$$\left[ \sum_1^n (I - t) + R_{ed} - MV_0 \right] = 0$$

where one takes the internal rate of return of the annual net of tax interest payments from year 1 to year $n$ plus the redemption payment in year $n$ minus the original market value of the debt in year 0. Interest and redemption payments are assumed to be payable at year end and tax to be immediately recoverable:

Using basic figures from (a) above together with $n = 5$ and $R_{ed} = 101$ the calculation is shown in Table 4.1.

Discounting at 5 per cent gives a positive NPV. Discounting again at 10 per cent gives a negative NPV. The internal rate of return, or cost of debt, is, therefore, between 5 per cent and 10 per cent. The actual cost is found by the process of interpolation to give:

$$r_d = 5 + \frac{9.487}{9.487 + 9.499} (10 - 5) \approx 7.498, \text{ say } 7.5\%$$

**Table 4.1** Calculation of the cost of redeemable debt

|  | Year | Cash flow | DF @ 5% | DF @ 10% | PV @ 5% | PV @ 10% |
|---|---|---|---|---|---|---|
| MV (ex interest) | 0 | 90 | 1.000 | 1.000 | (90.000) | (90.000) |
| $I - t$ | 1 to 5 | 7 (0.67) |  |  |  |  |
|  |  | = 4.69 | 4.329 | 3.791 | 20.303 | 17.780 |
| $R_{ed}$ | 5 | 101 | 0.784 | 0.621 | 79.184 | 62.721 |
|  |  |  |  |  | 9.487 | (9.499) |

## Cost of preference shares

The cost of preference share capital is related to the amount of dividend payable on the share.

The cost may be represented by:

$$\frac{d_0}{MV(\text{ex dividend})}$$

So, assuming a dividend of, say, 7p per £1 preference share and a market value of 60p (ex dividend):

$$r_p = \frac{7}{60} = 11.7\%$$

## Weighted average cost of capital (WACC)

The weighted average cost of capital (WACC) can be found by calculating the cost of each long-term source of finance weighted by the proportions of finance used. In theory, market values of the securities should be used in the gearing calculations as these give a more accurate measure of the company's value, although book values are frequently used in practice. Using market values for a firm with only two sources of finance, debt and equity, the WACC would be:

$$r_d \frac{V_d}{V_d + V_e} + r_e \frac{V_d}{V_d + V_e}$$

where $V_d$ and $V_e$ denote the market value of debt and equity respectively.

The following example shows how to calculate WACC for a company with three sources of finance: debt, equity and preference shares.

*Extracts from the balance sheet of XYZ plc*

|  | £ |
|---|---|
| Issued share capital: ordinary shares of 25p | 250,000 |
| Retained earnings | 350,000 |
| Undated 15% unsecured loan stock | 250,000 |
| Undated 7% preference shares of £1 each | 150,000 |
| Total financing | 1,000,000 |

The ordinary shares are currently quoted at 125p each, the loan stock is trading at £85 per £100 nominal and the preference shares at 65p each.

The market value of the securities is calculated in Table 4.2. If XYZ plc's cost of equity is 16 per cent and the company is a taxpayer, the WACC is calculated as shown in Table 4.3.

The cost of the loan stock and the preference shares are calculated as follows:

**Table 4.2** Calculation of market values

|  | Market value £ | % of total market value |
|---|---|---|
| Equity: | | |
| 1 million shares at 125p | 1,250,000 | 80.13 |
| Loan stock: | | |
| £250,000 @ £85 per £100 | 212,500 | 13.62 |
| Preference shares: | | |
| 150,000 shares at 65p | 97,500 | 6.25 |
| | 1,560,000 | 100.00 |

**Table 4.3** Weighted average cost of capital (based on market values)

| Source | % of capital (A) | Gross cost % | Tax @ 33% | After-tax cost % (B) | Weighted cost % (A × B) |
|---|---|---|---|---|---|
| Equity | 80.13 | 16.0 | | 16.0 | 12.82 |
| Loan stock | 13.62 | 17.6 | 5.8 | 11.8 | 1.61 |
| Preference | 6.25 | 10.8 | | 10.8 | 0.68 |
| | | | | | 15.11 |

Gross cost of loan stock

$$r_i = \frac{I}{MP} = \frac{15}{85} = 17.6\%$$

After-tax cost of loan stock

$$r_d = \frac{I(1-t)}{MP} = \frac{15(1-0.33)}{85} = 11.8\%$$

Cost of preference shares

$$r_p = \frac{DPS}{MPS}$$

$$= \frac{7}{65} = 10.8\%$$

We can work out the WACC using book values and compare our answer with the one given above. We must remember that the book value of equity includes retained earnings. The answer is as shown in Table 4.4.

WACC can be used as a cut-off or discounting rate for calculating the net present value of projected cash flows for new investments, but the following criteria should be met:

**Table 4.4** Weighted average cost of capital (book values)

| Source | % of capital (A) | Gross cost % | Tax @ 33% | After-tax cost % (B) | Weighted cost % (A × B) |
|---|---|---|---|---|---|
| Equity | 60.00 | 16.0 | | 16.0 | 9.60 |
| Loan stock | 25.00 | 17.6 | 5.8 | 11.8 | 2.95 |
| Preference | 15.00 | 10.8 | | 10.8 | 1.62 |
| | | | | | 14.17 |

- the capital structure is reasonably constant;
- the new investment does not carry a significantly different risk profile from that of the existing entity;
- the new investment does not require the introduction of new funds which can change the capital structure or its risk profile.

## MARGINAL COST OF CAPITAL

Use of WACC assumes that the capital structure of an entity will remain unchanged and that any new investment will have a similar risk profile to existing investments. If a large project is under consideration, and it would fundamentally affect the capital structure of an entity, these assumptions would mean that WACC is no longer the appropriate technique for investment appraisal. Use of WACC could lead to the acceptance of projects that reduce the entity's value.

The relevant cost of capital is now arguably the incremental cost, ie the marginal cost reflecting the changes in the total cost of the capital structure before and after the introduction of the new capital.

In theory, the marginal cost of capital is just the difference between the total cost with the existing capital structure and the total cost with the new capital structure once the investment has been undertaken. Consider a company with the following cost of capital as shown in Table 4.5.

**Table 4.5** Weighted average cost of capital

| Source | After-tax cost (%) A | Market value (£m) B | A × B |
|---|---|---|---|
| Equity | 20 | 5 | 1.00 |
| Preference | 10 | 1 | 0.10 |
| Loan stock | 8 | 4 | 0.32 |
| | | 10 | 1.42 |

WACC = 1.42/10 × 100 = 14.2%

It has under consideration a large investment project, to be financed by a major issue of funds which will alter the capital structure. The estimated project cost is £1,000,000, to be financed in equal proportions by a new share issue and a new issue of loan stock.

The new capital structure will imply a new level of risk for holders of loan stock and equity shares, causing the cost of capital for the company to change. The new cost of capital may be as shown in Table 4.6.

The total cost of capital has increased by £260,000 as a result of raising £1,000,000 of funds. The incremental cost of capital is, therefore, 26 per cent.

It might be thought that by raising £500,000 of equity with a cost of 22 per cent, and £500,000 of loan stock with a cost of 10 per cent, the marginal cost of capital would be:

$$(0.5 \times 22) + (0.5 \times 10) = 16\%$$

but this would ignore the change in the cost of original capital.

The approach illustrated here is appropriate only if the investment project is large relative to the current size of the entity, and undertaking the project causes an identifiable difference in the capital structure. In practice, companies rarely raise funds from a particular source for a particular purpose, which makes this approach difficult to use.

**Table 4.6** New weighted average cost of capital

| Source | After-tax cost (%) A | Market value (£m) B | A × B |
|---|---|---|---|
| Equity | 22 | 5.5 | 1.21 |
| Preference | 10 | 1.0 | 0.10 |
| Loan stock | 8 | 4.0 | 0.32 |
| New loan stock | 10 | 0.5 | 0.05 |
| | | 11.0 | 1.68 |

Weighted average cost of capital = $1.68/11 \times 100 = 15.3\%$

Marginal cost of capital = $1.68 - 1.42/11 - 10 \times 100 = 26\%$

## IDENTIFYING THE OPTIMAL CAPITAL STRUCTURE

Financial gearing may be defined as the 'use of debt to increase the expected return on equity'. This advantage to equity-holders arises from the *tax shield* on debt, ie the benefit to shareholders deriving from the treatment of debt for tax purposes as being deductible in arriving at an entity's taxable profits. High gearing means that debt represents a high proportion of the financing of an entity's assets, whereby in its capital structure of equity plus debt $(E + D)$, the element $D$ is high in proportion to the element $E$; conversely, low gearing is where $D$ is low in relation to $E$.

The main disadvantage of increasing debt is that the additional interest payable reduces the earnings available to shareholders, thereby increasing the risk of their investment and consequently increasing the cost of capital, as new investors will require a higher return on equity to compensate for the increased risk.

If you are still doubtful as to why increasing debt increases risk, you must appreciate that debt has priority over equity and also that coupon rates of debt must be met. Thus, if an entity hits bad times and profits fall significantly or losses ensue, there may be little if any return for shareholders. Clearly, therefore, the level of an entity's gearing can affect both earnings per share and dividend policy decisions.

The cost of a particular source of capital will depend on the risk associated with the source. We have stated that the overall cost of capital for a company is the weighted average of the costs of each individual source. In this section of the chapter we look at three views as to the impact that capital structure has on the cost of capital.

## TRADITIONAL THEORY OF GEARING

The traditional theory of financial gearing is based on the following assumptions:

- earnings remain constant in perpetuity and all investors have the same expectations about future earnings;
- taxation is ignored;
- risk remains constant, no matter how funds are invested;
- all earnings are paid out in dividends.

From Figure 4.1 we note that:

- cost of equity increases as level of gearing increases;
- as gearing level increases, cost of debt remains unchanged up to a certain point in the level of gearing, beyond which it will increase;
- WACC forms a type of U-shape, at first falling as level of debt increases and then tending to increase as rising equity costs (and perhaps rising cost of debt) become more significant.

The traditional view, therefore, is that WACC will be lowest at a level of gearing which represents an optimal capital structure (point *OCS* on the graph), which also aligns with the view that the capital structure that minimizes WACC will also be that which maximizes

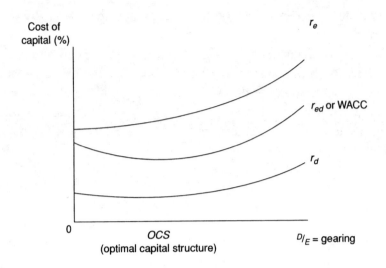

**Figure 4.1** Traditional theory of gearing

the value of the firm, always provided that we assume earnings to be independent of the capital structure. This can be illustrated as follows:

### Example

Mansel plc is expected to generate annual earnings of £600,000 for the foreseeable future. Ignoring taxation, calculate the total market value of Mansel plc, assuming that its cost of capital (WACC) is either (1) 10 per cent; or (2) 20 per cent.

### Solution

$$MV = \frac{\text{Earnings}}{r_{ed}} \quad \text{where } r_{ed} = \text{cost of capital (WACC)}$$

If $r_{ed} = 10\%$:

$$MV = \frac{600,000}{0.1} = £6,000,000$$

If $r_{ed} = 20\%$:

$$MV = \frac{600,000}{0.2} = £3,000,000$$

## *MODIGLIANI AND MILLER'S (MM) THEORIES OF GEARING*

The background to MM's 1958 theory, which forms the basis for the 'net operating income' view of WACC, is set out as follows.

Assuming the conditions apply of a perfect capital market, two companies which yield identical earnings and have similar risk profiles and production capabilities will have the same value in terms of capitalization whatever their capital structures may be.

MM also assume that taxation and transaction costs can be ignored, and that their assumptions are supported by market intervention through the process of 'arbitrage' whereby the actions of investors would equate the values of the two companies in all respects except that of leverage (the use of debt, which is assumed to be risk-free and costs the same to individuals as to companies, to increase the expected return on equity). 'Arbitraging' here refers to the switching of funds by an investor as between investments in order to obtain a better return for the same risk level, and is explained in the next section.

In the perfect capital market assumed by MM, information is freely available to all investors who, in turn, are assumed to act rationally, to have similar expectations as to returns and also to be in agreement as to the expected future streams of earning for each company, while all companies can be classified into equivalent risk groups. From this background, MM set out their three propositions.

### *Proposition I*

'The market value of any firm is independent of its capital structure and is given by capitalizing its expected return at the rate appropriate to its class.' This can also be expressed in terms of a firm's 'average cost of capital', which is the ratio of the expected return to the market value of all its securities; thus, 'the average cost of capital to any firm is completely independent of its capital structure, and is equal to the capitalization rate of a pure equity stream of its class'.

## Proposition II

This relates to the rate of return on equity in companies whose capital structure includes some debt: 'The expected yield of a share of stock is equal to the appropriate capitalization rate for a pure equity stream in the class, plus a premium related to financial risk equal to the debt-to-equity ratio times the spread between [the capitalization rate and the interest rate on debt]'.

In simpler terms, these two propositions have the following effects:

1. The total market value of a company is independent of the level of debt in its capital structure. This value can be calculated by capitalizing the expected flow of operational earnings (before interest payments) at an appropriate discount rate depending on risk category.
2. As leverage (use of debt) increases, the equity cost of capital to a levered company will also rise in order to exactly offset the advantages accruing from the lower cost of debt relative to equity. Note that debt is cheaper than equity, owing to its carrying a lower risk – or even a risk-free profile – in that payment of interest on debt and usually repayment of principal (say, in a breaking up of the company) takes precedence over equity dividends or repayment.

## Proposition III

This provides a rule for optimal investment policy by the firm: 'The cut-off point for investment in the firm will in all cases be [the average cost of capital] and will be completely unaffected by the type of security used to finance the investment'.

So, if the first two propositions hold, the cut-off rate used to evaluate investments will not be affected by the type of funding used to finance them, whatever may be the capital structure. The gain from using debt (at lower cost) is offset by the increased cost of equity (due to increased risk) and WACC, therefore, remains constant. In order to maximize equity-holders' wealth, the company should, therefore, use its WACC as a cut-off rate.

These arguments are not easy to grasp for those who are new to the subject. To help your understanding, here is how Propositions I and II are stated in a standard text on this subject (Brealey *et al*, 1996):

[MM's] famous 'Proposition I' states that a firm cannot change the *total* value of its securities just by splitting its cash flows into different streams: the firm's value is determined by its real assets, not by the securities it issues. Thus, capital structure is irrelevant as long as the firm's investment decisions are taken as given.

This is MM's Proposition II: The expected rate of return on the common stock of a levered firm increases in proportion to the debt–equity ratio ($D/E$), expressed in market values; the rate of increase depends on the spread between $r_A$, the expected rate of return on a portfolio of all the firm's securities, and $r_D$, the expected return on the debt. Note that $r_E = r_A$ if the firm has no debt.

Note from Figure 4.2 that at the higher levels of gearing, there is the apparent paradox of cost of equity falling and cost of debt rising. This is explained by the selling of equity by existing shareholders who are relatively risk-averse, to other investors who are prepared to take much higher risks for the possibility of a high return; the effect is to reduce the cost of equity at the same time that the cost of debt, now perceived by its holders as being increasingly risky, will carry an increasing cost.

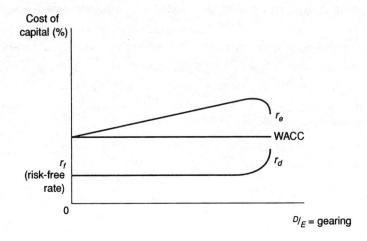

**Figure 4.2** MM's gearing propositions without tax

The three propositions may be expressed as equations as follows:

Proposition I

$$V_g = V_{ug}$$

where

$V_g$ = value of geared company
$V_{ug}$ = value of ungeared company

Proposition II

$$r_{eg} = r_{eu} + D/E \, (r_{eu} - r_d)$$

where

$r_{eg}$ = cost of equity in geared company
$r_{eu}$ = cost of equity in ungeared company
$r_d$ = cost of debt (gross of tax)
$E$ = market value of equity
$D$ = market value of debt

Proposition III

$$WACC_g = WACC_{ug} = r_{eu}$$

where

$WACC_g$ = cost of capital in geared company
$WACC_{ug}$ = cost of capital in ungeared company

## Example

X plc is identical in all operating and risk characteristics to Y plc, except that X plc is all equity financed and Y plc is financed by equity valued at £2.1 million and debt valued at £0.9 million based on market values. The interest paid on Y plc's debt is £72,000 per annum, and it pays a dividend to shareholders of £378,000 per annum. X plc pays an annual dividend of £450,000.

## Required

(i)   Identify the value of X plc;
(ii)  Calculate the cost of capital for X plc;
(iii) Calculate the cost of equity for Y plc;
(iv)  Calculate the cost of debt for Y plc;
(v)   Calculate the weighted average cost of capital for Y plc.

## Solution

(i)  The diagrams as shown in Figure 4.3 below represent the balance sheets of X plc and Y plc in the form of a square. The left-hand side reflects the sources of finance, shown as equity ($E$) for X plc and a mix of equity ($E$) and debt ($D$) for Y plc. The right-hand side reflects how those sources have been applied in the form of assets ($A$).

(ii)

$$r_{eu} = \frac{\text{Dividend}}{E} = \frac{450}{3,000} = 0.15 = 15\%$$

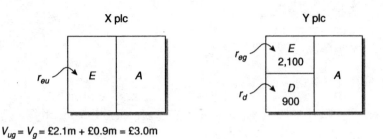

$$V_{ug} = V_g = \text{£}2.1\text{m} + \text{£}0.9\text{m} = \text{£}3.0\text{m}$$

**Figure 4.3** Square balance sheets

(iii)

$$r_{eg} = r_{eu} + \frac{D}{E}(r_{eu} - r_d)$$

$$= 15\% + \frac{900}{2,100}(15 - 8) = 18\%$$

Alternatively

$$r_{eg} = \frac{\text{Dividend}}{E} = \frac{378}{2,100} = 0.18 = 18\%$$

(iv)

$$r_d = \frac{\text{Interest}}{D} = \frac{72}{900} = 0.08 = 8\%$$

(v)

$$\text{WACC}_g = r_d\frac{D}{D + E} + r_{eg}\frac{E}{D + E}$$

$$= 0.08 \times \frac{900}{3,000} + 0.18 \times \frac{2,100}{3,000}$$

$$= \frac{450}{3,000} = 15\% = \text{WACC}_{ug}$$

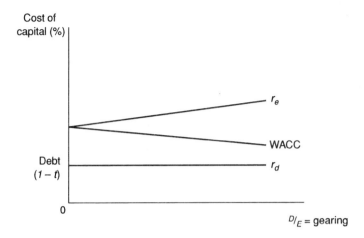

**Figure 4.4** MM's gearing propositions with tax

In 1963, MM accepted that corporate taxation could indeed have a distorting effect, in that as a result of debt interest being deductible before computing taxation, WACC would continuously decrease as additional amounts of debt were incorporated into the company's capital structure. This is illustrated in Figure 4.4.

The formulae from above may be amended for the impact of tax as follows:

Proposition I

$$V_g = V_{ug} + PV_{ts}$$

where

$V_g$ = value of geared company
$V_{ug}$ = value of ungeared company
$PV_{ts}$ = present value of tax shield

Proposition II

$$r_{eg} = r_{eu} + (r_{eu} - r_d)(1 - t)\frac{D}{E}$$

where

$r_{eg}$ = cost of equity in geared company
$r_{eu}$ = cost of equity in ungeared company
$r_d$ = cost of debt (gross of tax)
$E$ = market value of equity
$D$ = market value of debt
$t$ = corporation tax rate.

Proposition III

$$WACC_g = r_{eu} - \left[ \frac{r_{eu}Dt}{D + E} \right]$$

or

$$WACC_g = \left[ r_{eg} \times \frac{E}{D + E} \right] + \left[ r_d(1 - t) \frac{D}{D + E} \right]$$

where

$WACC_g$ = cost of capital in geared company

For this proposition our assumptions change to allow for the inclusion of the debt tax relief at 33 per cent as follows. The value of Y plc will increase as shown in Figure 4.5.

$$V_g = V_{ug} + PV_{ts}$$
$$= 3,000,000 + (900,000 \times 0.33)$$
$$= £3,297,000$$

The value of equity for Y plc becomes

$$= V_g - D$$
$$= £3,297,000 - £900,000$$
$$= £2,397,000$$

The cost of equity for Y plc is now calculated as:

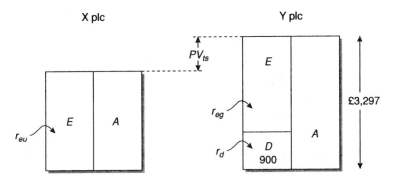

**Figure 4.5** Balance sheets of X plc and Y plc

$$r_{eg} = r_{eu} + \left[ (1 - t) \frac{D}{E} (r_{eu} - r_d) \right]$$

$$= 15\% + \left[ 0.67 \times \frac{900}{2,397} (15\% - 8\%) \right]$$

$$= 15\% + 1.76\% = 16.76\%$$

The weighted average cost of capital now becomes:

$$\text{WACC}_g = r_{eu} - \left[ \frac{r_{eu} Dt}{D + E} \right] = 15 - \left[ \frac{15 \times 900 \times 0.33}{3,297} \right] \approx 13.65\%$$

or

$$\text{WACC}_g = \left[ r_{eg} \times \frac{E}{D + E} \right] + \left[ r_d (1 - t) \frac{D}{D + E} \right]$$

$$= \left[ 16.76\% \times \frac{2,397}{3,297} \right] + \left[ 8\% \times 0.67 \times \frac{900}{3,297} \right]$$

$$\approx 13.65\%$$

Apart from MM's own recognition of a flaw in their basic theory as examined above, other limitations can be briefly mentioned as follows:

- cost of capital is not likely to remain constant in the real world;
- personal and corporate leverage are seldom equivalent, for companies even of medium size are likely to have a higher credit rating than most individual investors;
- most investors would face less risk if they allow a company with limited liability to borrow on their behalf;
- very high levels of gearing carry considerable dangers of corporate collapse.

## HOW ARBITRAGE WORKS WITHIN A TAX ENVIRONMENT

Assume two companies, $V_{ug}$ – which is ungeared – and $V_g$ – which has £1.1 million of undated debt with a coupon rate of 8 per cent valued at par. Earnings before interest and tax are £600,000 in perpetuity for both companies, and tax is 33 per cent. Taking the traditional view, we could have a position as shown in Table 4.7 (assuming all after-tax earnings are paid as dividends).

**Table 4.7** Earnings and value of ungeared and geared companies

|  | $V_{ug}$ £000 | $V_g$ £000 |
|---|---|---|
| Earnings before interest and tax | 600 | 600 |
| Interest | – | (88) |
|  | 600 | 512 |
| Tax (33%) | (198) | (169) |
| Dividends | 402 | 343 |
| Value of equity | 3,013 | 2,400 |
| Value of debt | – | 1,100 |
|  | 3,013 | 3,500 |

Assuming $V_{ug}$'s shares are in equilibrium, according to MM:

$$V_g = V_{ug} + PV_{ts}$$
$$= 3,013 + (1,100 \times 0.33)$$
$$= £3,376,000$$

But $V_g$ actually = £3,500,000 – ie it is overvalued. Investors in $V_g$ could do better by selling their shares and buying shares in $V_{ug}$.

SG is an investor holding 2 per cent of $V_g$'s equity, yielding an income of £6,860 (ie £343,000 × 2%). To maximize reward in relation to risk the investor should now proceed as follows:

(a) sell holding in $V_g$ for £48,000 (ie £2.4m × 2%);
(b) assume the same financial risk as $V_g$ by borrowing an amount equal to 2 per cent of $V_g$'s debt, adjusted to allow for tax relief (ie 2% × £1,100,000 × 0.67 = £14,740);
(c) now buy £62,740 (£48,000 + £14,740) of $V_{ug}$'s equity, to earn greater income than before.

| | £ |
|---|---|
| Dividends from $V_{ug}$: 402,000 × 62,740/3,013,000 | 8,371 |
| Less interest on personal debt: 14,740 × 8% | (1,179) |
| | 7,192 |

Thus, SG can increase his income by (7,192 – 6,860) = £332 for the same level of risk. But:

- the actions in the market will very quickly erode this advantage so that $V_g$'s equity will fall in price and the price of $V_{ug}$'s equity will increase, until an equilibrium point is reached when $V_g$ will again equal $V_{ug} + PV_{ts}$;
- at the equilibrium point, the cost of equity $r_e$ will be higher for $V_g$ than for $V_{ug}$.

As $V_g$ = £3,376,000 the value of the equity is represented by:

$$V_{ug} = V_g - D$$
$$= \pounds3,376,000 - \pounds1,100,000$$
$$= \pounds2,276,000$$

The cost of equity is calculated as:

$$r_{eg} = \frac{343}{2,276} = 15.07\%$$

The cost of equity for $V_{ug}$ the ungeared company is:

$$r_{eu} = \frac{402}{3,013} = 13.4\% \text{ as stated}$$

which demonstrates that the cost of equity $r_e$ will be higher for $V_g$ than for $V_{ug}$.

## SUMMARY

In the first part of this chapter we examined methods of assessing the costs of equity, preference shares and debt finance. We also explored the impact that capital structure has on the overall cost of capital for an organization as measured by the weighted average cost of capital.

Internal constraints to policy formulation and action centre mainly on funding and gearing. In the second part of this chapter we have traced basic financial theories of the value of an entity through the traditional view and the propositions of Modigliani and Miller. These theories should be viewed as a starting point for appreciating the problems faced by the treasury manager in determining the most appropriate capital structure for the organization.

The main argument for gearing is that by introducing debt, the interest payments attract tax relief. The main argument against debt is that it also introduces financial risk into a company. These are factors which call for the treasury manager to formulate a policy which will effectively balance out their opposing effects.

# 5

# Dividend Policy

Dividend policy is one of a company's financing decisions. Ideally, a company should have either a policy on distributions or a policy on retentions. Potential equity investors are then more aware of the implications of investing in the company. A decision must be made between making payments to shareholders and retaining funds for future investment. Using internally generated funds is often thought to be a free form of finance. This, however, is not the case because retained funds have a cost: the opportunity cost of a dividend foregone.

## *FACTORS AFFECTING DIVIDEND POLICY*

In deciding a company's dividend policy the following factors should be considered:

- *Liquidity* In order to pay dividends, a company will require access to cash. Even very profitable companies may sometimes have difficulty paying dividends if resources are tied up in other forms of asset, especially if bank overdraft facilities are not available.
- *Repayment of debt* Dividend pay-out may be made difficult if debt is scheduled for repayment and this is not financed by a further issue of funds.
- *Restrictive covenants* The Articles of Association may contain agreed restrictions on dividends. In addition, some forms of debt may have restrictive covenants limiting the

amount of dividend payments or the rate of growth which applies to them.

- *Rate of expansion*   The funds may be needed to avoid over-trading.
- *Stability of profits*   Other things being equal, a company with stable profits is more likely to be able to pay out a higher percentage of earnings than a company with fluctuating profits.
- *Control*   The use of retained earnings to finance new projects preserves the company's ownership and control. This can be advantageous in firms where the present disposition of shareholdings is of importance.
- *Policy of competitors*   Dividend policies of competitors may influence corporate dividend policy. It may be difficult, for example, to reduce a dividend for the sake of further investment, when competitors follow a policy of higher distributions.
- *Signalling effect*   This is the information content of dividends. Dividends are seen as signals from the company to the financial markets and shareholders. Investors perceive dividend announcements as signals of future prospects for the company. This aspect of dividend policy is assuming increasing importance, and there have been numerous instances reported in the press where companies have paid an increased dividend when financial prudence suggests they should be paying no dividend at all.

Having taken into account the above factors, companies will formulate standard dividend policies, three of which are discussed below.

### Constant pay-out ratio

There are important links between dividends and profits. In company law, for instance, the prohibition of paying dividends other than out of profits is seen as an important protection for creditors (including lenders, who may well specify a maximum proportion of profits which can be declared as dividends while their loans remain in force). This is reinforced by the accounting concept which defines profit as what you could afford to distribute, and still be as well off as you were. Such links encourage a backward-looking approach to dividend policy, with some boards of directors publishing an objective to maintain a certain dividend cover, ie to declare *dividends which represent a constant percentage of profits* after tax.

In a stable state, one would expect some symmetry in the figures, eg a company whose profits after tax represented a 10 per cent per annum return may choose to plough half back into the business, and look forward to a 5 per cent per annum growth in its profits (and earnings per share) and hence dividends. This forms the basis of the idea that the value of a company is a multiple of its past profits. The reality, however, is not one of a stable state.

One very specific shock to the system has been the instability of the unit of measure (money). Should dividends be related to the profits calculated under the historical cost convention, or after making an adjustment to exclude the inflationary element? Ought they to be influenced by translation gains and losses (usually taken direct to the reserves figure on the balance sheet)? Bear in mind that well-offness is measured by reference to the cost of unconsumed tangible assets. No allowance is made for the intangible assets (like quality, reputation and pace of innovation) which are so crucial to survival in a rapidly changing environment. Intriguingly, what the accountant calls an asset, eg an old-fashioned piece of plant, can actually be a strategic liability.

### Stable policy with 'moderate' pay-out

Other boards of directors think, not in terms of maintaining dividend cover, but in terms of maintaining a trend in the absolute level of pay-out. Their starting point for deciding this year's dividend is what was paid last year, what rate of increase it represented on the previous year and whether they feel that this rate can be repeated, taking into account considerations of liquidity. Rightly or wrongly, the dividend decision is seen as a powerful signal to the market, of the directors' confidence in the future of the enterprise, and this does appear to be supported by evidence that unexpected dividend cuts have been followed by a reduction in share prices. The danger, of course, is that this can become a game, in which directors seek to give the signal they think will have the most favourable effect on the share price. Some even argue that the aim must not be to surprise the market, which leads to the suggestion that the dividend should be what the analysts are predicting. As analysts base their predictions on confidential briefings by directors, however, such an incestuous approach is clearly irrational.

The last few years have seen a significant increase in the proportion of corporate profits being declared as dividends. Dividend cover (the ratio of profits after tax to dividends) was over 2.5 in the 1970s and 80s, but fell to below 2.0 in the early 1990s. In pure economic terms, this is to be applauded, in the sense that it puts the funds in the hands of those with the widest choice, and forces the directors to 'make a case' if they wish to raise capital to fund expansion. Conversely, the dividend controls which have been applied at various times in the past (usually to signal fairness, *vis-à-vis* wages and price controls) have a stultifying effect on the economy – preventing funds from following their natural course.

The practice of maintaining a particular rate (sometimes real, sometimes nominal) of growth of dividends has been very popular, and seemed to work well as long as things were stable, cyclical or at least predictable – enough being 'squirrelled away' in the good years to pay for the bad. As the rate of change has speeded up, however, its limitations have become more obvious and more serious. In particular, the unexpectedly severe downturn in the early 1990s presented such boards with a dilemma: given sharply reduced profits, what should be preserved – dividend growth or dividend cover?

Some of the fund managers made it clear that they preferred dividends to retentions. Some boards responded, to the point of declaring dividends in excess of their profits after tax. One chairperson talked about the need to 'reward shareholders for their loyalty'. As a general rule, however, financial journalists took the opposite view, based on their perception of dividends as just another outlay, like wages, or advertising, or plant and machinery. Companies in financial difficulties, they argued, should cut dividends and increase investment. Such comments give the impression that their authors mistakenly see financial management as about trade-offs within one time frame (ie the short term). The reality is that it is about trade-offs between different time frames: the investments financed by reduced dividends could well amount to a total waste of money.

### *Residual dividend policy*

If a company has opportunities to invest for a return in excess of the cost of capital, it should retain funds within the business. If, on the other hand, it has funds in excess of its identifiable viable investment opportunities, it should return them to its shareholders for investment elsewhere. This would mean much more volatile levels of dividend, of course, but that was what equity capital was originally meant to be about. The idea of a share being more like a bond, ie carrying an entitlement to a steady, or steadily increasing, stream of dividends, is relatively new. It may be coincidence, but it has come to prominence as the proportion of shares owned by institutions has grown. In the 1950s two-thirds of UK listed company shares were owned by individuals; by 1990, two-thirds were owned by institutions.

At this stage, it is worth noting that, rather than transferring wealth from the company to the shareholders in the form of dividends, it is possible to return capital to them by 'buying back shares', ie the company makes an offer to all members, or goes out into the market to buy its own shares. This does not happen very often but does allow shareholders to choose: they can take the cash, or have a larger interest in the company. The effect on the entity is the same as paying a dividend, but the tax situation may make it possible to benefit (at least some) shareholders at the expense of the tax authorities.

## *THEORY OF DIVIDEND IRRELEVANCY*

To appreciate the theory advanced by Modigliani and Miller (MM) in 1961 regarding dividend policy and the hypothesis of dividend irrelevance, we need to understand MM's fundamental principle of valuation, 'that the price of each share must be such that the rate of return (dividends plus capital gains per dollar invested) on every share will be the same throughout the market over any given interval of time'. This principle is supported by three basic assumptions:

1. In 'perfect capital' markets no buyer, seller or issuer of securities is large enough for their transactions to significantly affect the current ruling price. Information regarding the ruling price is available to all without cost and no brokerage fees, transfer taxes or other transaction costs are incurred in the trading of securities, also no tax differentials exist either between dividends or retentions of profit or between dividend and capital gains.
2. All investors will behave 'rationally' in that they will prefer more wealth to less, and they are indifferent as to whether any given increment of their wealth is in the form of cash payments (dividends) or an increase in the market value of their holdings (capital gains).
3. 'Perfect certainty' carries the implication of complete assurance on the part of every investor as to the future investment programme and future profits of every company. With this assurance there is, among other things, no need to distinguish between stocks and bonds as sources of funds for this analysis, which is itself based on an analytical framework set up to examine the effects of differences in dividend policy on the current price of shares in an ideal economy, characterized by the three assumptions of perfect capital markets, rational behaviour and perfect certainty.

Important aspects of this theory arising from the above assumptions, or developed from them, include the following:

- In a tax-free world, shareholders will not differentiate between dividends or capital gains, the value of a company and, therefore, the price of its shares being based only on the earnings capacity of its assets and investments, ie on the worth of the projects in which the company has invested its funds.
- The so-called 'clientele effect' shows that a company with a particular pattern and stability of dividend profile will attract stockholders having a similar preference for that type of profile, thus, since the expectations of the shareholders are being met, the price of shares will be unaffected by changes in dividend policy.
- If retentions are insufficient to allow a company to take up all its worthwhile investments, the shortfall caused by a dividend can be offset by obtaining further funds from other external sources. MM argue that, although there will be a loss in value of existing shares as a result of using external finance instead of retentions, such loss will be exactly offset by the amount of the dividend paid; as a result, a company should be indifferent as to whether it pays a dividend and obtains external funding or retains more of its profits. Thus the effect of dividends on share price is exactly compensated for by other sources of financing.
- MM recognize that dividends can in some way affect share prices, but suggest that the positive effects of dividend increases on such prices relate not to the dividend itself but to the 'informational content' of dividends in regard to future earnings. This information leads to shareholders pushing up the share price on the basis of their expectations as to future earnings.
- From these arguments it seems reasonable to assume that if a company does not have sufficient worthwhile projects to use up retentions, it should distribute these surplus funds to its shareholders, who will then be able to invest in other companies which do have satisfactory investments to which these extra funds can be applied.

Within the considerable limitations of the assumptions made, which are discussed below, MM do present some interesting, if contentious, arguments as to why dividends are irrelevant to the value of any particular company.

Has MM's theory any practical relevance today? Arguably, we can answer positively in that: (1) it sets out a number of issues which provide useful background in developing an approach to dividend policy, eg concerning 'informational content' of dividends; and (2) since legalization of share buy-backs in the UK, a number of companies have shown interest in, and a few have acted upon, the concept of returning surplus funds to shareholders, signifying that this may prove to be the better way of ensuring their more profitable use.

In a perfect world, which in the interests of clarity MM explicitly assumed, their theory would seem unexceptional. In the real world, however, we need to recognize some imperfections:

- Use of the accounting model for purposes beyond its design specification. As mentioned above, retention of profits is likely to result in the company reporting earnings per share growth. Paying dividends and raising capital would not. If that earnings per share figure is seen as a measure of performance, or is used for determining rewards, this could have considerable significance.
- Transaction costs. It costs money to pay a dividend, and it costs money to raise capital. To eliminate one transaction by reducing the size of the other would clearly avoid wasteful administration costs.
- Taxation is never neutral, and the declaration of a dividend can affect the attribution of value as between shareholders and the tax gatherers.
- Whether companies need be concerned about the tax ultimately borne by their shareholders – in respect of dividends and/or the buying and selling of shares – is a moot point. Some are adopting policies which appeal to a particular clientele, ie category of investor; others are passively watching

the steady decline of the individual shareholder, and the growth of the tax-exempt fund. Barring a change of policy, the UK market is polarizing: individuals are being encouraged to invest in National Savings and tax-exempt Individual Savings Accounts (ISAs); share ownership increasingly appeals only to pension funds and the like.

- The inefficiency of the market. A dividend is certain, being tangible cash in the hand and discretionary income, whereas the market price is subject to all sorts of extraneous influences and, therefore, more uncertain. Note, accordingly, how increasing the dividend is a predictable response to a threat of a take-over, the presumption being that it will have the effect of increasing the share price.

- Supporters of the efficient market hypothesis would like to think that prices equate with the net present value of projected cash flows and are, therefore, fair as between buyers and sellers, but it would be perverse to argue that directors have a responsibility for the bargains struck between consenting shareholders, ie for ensuring that reality fits the hypothesis! It would be more rational to argue that they should concentrate on creating wealth, and recognize that the question of its distribution as between stakeholders is far from being within their control.

## SCRIP DIVIDENDS

Changes to the UK taxation system from 6 April 1999 have had a significant impact on dividend policy. Prior to this date, the payment of a cash dividend by a company would trigger a requirement to pay advance corporation tax (ACT). The ACT paid could be recovered against the mainstream corporation tax liability for the year in which the dividend was paid, subject to a maximum annual offset. ACT was abolished as from 6 April 1999.

Prior to the abolition of ACT many companies gave their shareholders a choice between a cash dividend and additional shares worth the same, or approximately the same, amount. Companies were not required to pay ACT on dividends paid in shares, ie *scrip dividends*.

To see how this worked, imagine a company with 100 million shares in issue, whose directors decided to declare a dividend of 12p per share. In the 'normal' course of events, this would have meant a cash outflow of £12 million to the shareholders and £3 million to the Inland Revenue in the form of ACT. Assuming, for the sake of illustration, that the company's shares had been trading at around 360p ex dividend, the board might have offered an alternative of one new share for every 30 held. There would have been rules as to fractional entitlements, of course, but in simple terms someone who held, say, 3,000 shares could have had a dividend of £360, or 100 shares' worth – at the contemporary share price – £360.

Directors tended to encourage shareholders to take the shares rather than the cash. By doing so, as one company chairperson argued in a report, 'there is a benefit to the company (and, there-fore, to the shareholders) from the retention of cash that would otherwise be paid out in dividends and ACT'. Implicit in that argu-ment, it should be noted, is the presumption that the retained funds will be invested in projects which can reasonably be expected to earn an adequate return. As with 'bonus issues', directors rarely highlight the fact that, once the reserves are capitalized in this way, they become undistributable. From the point of view of individual shareholders:

- if they had been thinking of buying some more shares, and felt that the price was unlikely to fall below 360p in the near future, they would welcome the opportunity of obtaining some without having to pay the usual commissions etc;
- if they had no wish to increase their holding, they could simply take the dividend as originally declared;
- if they had no firm views, they could take part dividend and part shares.

The choice was left to the individual, with as little bias as is feasible given the inevitable fluctuations in share prices. If there were benefits to the company, they did not accrue to the individual choosing the scrip, but were shared across the entire register. Not surprisingly, therefore, the take-up of the scrip alternative, on this basis, tended to be very light.

But then came a variant: the *enhanced* scrip option. The idea here was to offer shareholders the alternative of a significantly higher number of shares than would equate with the value of the dividend. The company in our earlier example may offer, for example, a choice between a 12p dividend and, not one share for 30, but one for 20. Someone owning 3,000 shares, in other words, had a choice between £360 in cash or shares worth – at the contemporary price – £540. Just in case they did not get the message, it would be simultaneously announced that a friendly merchant bank was prepared to buy any of these shares for, say, 353p each for resale in the market. Needless to say, the take-up on these schemes was almost total.

During 1998 many companies announced the withdrawal of their scrip dividend schemes in advance of the taxation changes announced for April 1999, which would remove many of the attractions of these schemes. Many companies also announced a rescheduling of their cash dividends to become payable after 6 April 1999 in order to avoid an ACT liability.

## *SUMMARY*

Dividend payments have been shown to be irrelevant to shareholder wealth in perfect capital markets. When market imperfections – such as taxes, transaction costs and imperfect information – are considered, the situation is less clear. Companies tend to adopt stable and consistent dividend policies in order to attract a clientele of investors whose personal taxation position suits that particular policy. Unexpected fluctuations in the dividend payment tend to be avoided because of the informational content of the dividend which is being signalled to the market.

# 6

# Working Capital Management

In this chapter we look first at the overall management of working capital and then progress to look more closely at the individual components of debtors, stock, creditors and cash.

## *INTRODUCTION*

Working capital is generally defined as 'the capital available for conducting the day-to-day operations of an organization'. In accounting terms, this is a static balance sheet concept, referring to the excess – at a particular moment in time – of permanent capital plus long-term liabilities over the fixed assets of the business. As such, it depends on accounting rules, such as what is capital and what is revenue, what constitutes a retained profit, the cut-off between long term and short term (12 months from the balance sheet date for published accounts) and when revenue should be recognized.

If working capital, thus defined, exceeds net current operating assets (stocks plus debtors less creditors) the company has a cash surplus (usually represented by bank deposits and investments); otherwise it has a deficit (usually represented by a bank loan and/or overdraft).

A business must be able to generate sufficient cash to be able to meet its immediate obligations and, therefore, continue trading. Unprofitable businesses can survive for quite some time if they have access to sufficient liquid resources, but even the most profitable business will quickly go under if it does not have adequate liquid resources. Working capital is, therefore, essential to the company's long-term success and development, and the greater the degree to which the current assets cover the current liabilities, the more solvent the company.

The efficient management of working capital is important from the point of view of both liquidity and profitability. Poor management of working capital means that funds are unnecessarily tied up in idle assets, hence reducing liquidity and also reducing the ability to invest in productive assets such as plant and machinery, so affecting profitability.

## *WORKING CAPITAL POLICY*

A company's working capital policy is a function of two decisions. First, the appropriate level of investment in, and mix of current assets to be decided upon, for a set level of activity. This is the *investment decision*. Second, the methods of financing this investment – the *financing decision*.

### *The investment decision*

In conditions of uncertainty firms must hold some minimal level of cash and inventories based on expected sales, plus additional safety stocks. With an *aggressive working capital* policy, a firm would hold minimal safety stock. Such a policy would minimize costs, but it could lower sales because the firm may not be able to respond rapidly to increases in demand.

Conversely, a *conservative working capital* policy would call for large safety stocks. Generally, the expected return is lower under a conservative than under an aggressive policy, but the risks are greater under the aggressive policy. A *moderate* policy falls somewhere between the two extremes in terms of risk and returns.

## The financing decision

Working capital financing decisions involve the determination of the mix of long-term versus short-term debt. When the yield curve is upward-sloping, short-term debt costs less than long-term debt.

With an aggressive financing policy, the firm finances part of its permanent asset base with short-term debt. This policy generally provides the highest expected return (because short-term debt costs are typically less than long-term costs) but it is very risky.

Under a conservative financing policy, the firm would have permanent financing (long-term debt plus equity) which exceeds its permanent base of assets. The conservative policy is the least risky but also results in the lowest expected return. The maturity matching policy falls between the two extremes.

There is a basic difference between cash and inventories, on the one hand, and receivables on the other. In the case of cash and inventories, higher levels mean safety stock, hence a more conservative position. There is no such thing as a 'safety stock of receivables', and a higher level of receivables in relation to sales would generally mean that the firm was extending credit on more liberal terms. If we characterize aggressive as being risky, then lowering inventories and cash would be aggressive but raising receivables would also be aggressive.

The financing of working capital depends upon how current and fixed asset funding is divided between long-term and short-term sources of funding. Three possible policies exist as shown in Figures 6.1, 6.2 and 6.3.

A conservative policy is where all of the permanent assets – both fixed assets and the permanent part of the current assets (ie the core level of investment in stocks and debtors etc) – is financed by long-term funding, as well as part of the fluctuating current assets. Short-term financing is only used for part of the fluctuating current assets.

An aggressive policy for financing working capital uses short-term financing to fund all the fluctuating current assets as well as

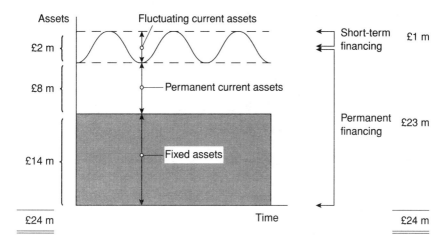

**Figure 6.1** Conservative financing policy

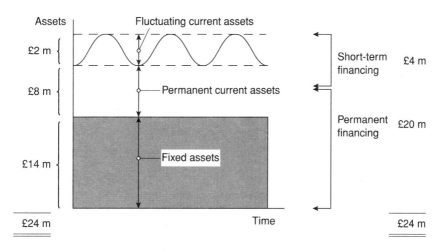

**Figure 6.2** Aggressive financing policy

some of the permanent part of the current assets. This policy carries the greatest risk of illiquidity, as well as the greatest returns.

A moderate policy matches the short-term finance to the fluctuating current assets, and the long-term finance to the permanent part of current assets plus fixed assets.

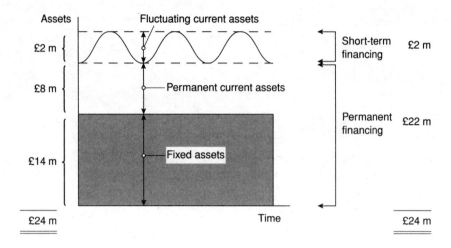

**Figure 6.3** Moderate financing policy

## THE OPERATING CYCLE

The operating cycle is the length of time between the company's outlay on raw materials, wages and other expenditures, and the inflow of cash from the sale of the goods. In a manufacturing business this is the average time that raw materials remain in stock, less the period of credit taken from suppliers, plus the time taken for producing the goods, plus the time the goods remain in finished inventory, plus the time taken by customers to pay for the goods. On some occasions this cycle is referred to as the cash cycle.

This is an important concept for the management of cash or working capital because the longer the operating cycle the more financial resource the company needs. Management needs to watch that this cycle does not become too long. The operating cycle can be calculated approximately as shown in Tables 6.1, 6.2 and 6.3 and the calculation below. Allowances should be made for any significant changes in the level of stocks taking place over the period. If, for example, the company is deliberately building up its level of stocks, this will lengthen the operating cycle.

**Table 6.1** Calculation of the operating cycle

| Raw materials | | Days |
|---|---|---|
| Period of turnover of raw materials stock | average value of raw material stock / purchase of raw materials per day | x |
| Less: Period of credit granted by suppliers | average level of creditors / purchase of raw materials per day | (x) |
| Period of production | average value of work in progress / average cost of goods sold per day | x |
| Period of turnover of finished goods stock | average value of stock of finished goods / average cost of goods sold per day | x |
| Period of credit taken by customers | average value of debtors / average value of sales per day | x |
| Total operating cycle | | X |

Some writers advocate computation of an annual operating cycle and of a cycle for each quarter, since with a seasonal business the cycle would vary over different periods. The numerators in the equations can be found by taking the arithmetic mean of the opening and closing balances for stocks, creditors and debtors. If a quarterly statement is being prepared, the opening and closing balances for the quarter would be used.

### Example

Table 6.2 below gives information extracted from the annual accounts of Davis plc for the past two years. Calculate the length of the operating cycle for each of the two years.

The operating cycle for Davis plc will be calculated as shown in Table 6.3 below.

Note that, owing to the nature of the simplified information provided, end-of-year values – rather than average values – have been used for stocks, debtors and creditors.

**Table 6.2** Davis plc – Extracts from annual accounts

|  | Year 1 £ | Year 2 £ |
|---|---|---|
| Stocks: Raw materials | 108,000 | 145,800 |
| Work-in-progress | 75,600 | 97,200 |
| Finished goods | 86,400 | 129,600 |
| Purchases | 518,400 | 702,000 |
| Cost of goods sold | 756,000 | 972,000 |
| Sales | 864,000 | 1,080,000 |
| Debtors | 172,800 | 259,200 |
| Trade creditors | 86,400 | 105,300 |

**Table 6.3** Calculation of operating cycle for Davis plc

|  | Year 1 % | Year 1 Days | Year 2 % | Year 2 Days |
|---|---|---|---|---|
| Raw materials stockholding (raw materials stock ÷ purchases) | 20.83 | 76 | 20.77 | 76 |
| *Less*: Finance from suppliers (trade creditors ÷ purchases) | 16.67 | 61 | 15.00 | 55 |
|  |  | 15 |  | 21 |
| Production time (work-in-progress ÷ cost of sales) | 10.00 | 37 | 10.00 | 37 |
| Finished goods stockholding (finished goods stock ÷ cost of sales) | 11.43 | 42 | 13.33 | 49 |
| Credit given to customers (debtors ÷ sales) | 20.00 | 73 | 24.00 | 88 |
|  |  | 167 |  | 195 |

A number of steps could be taken to shorten the operating cycle. The volume of debtor balances could be cut by a quicker collection of debt; finished goods could be turned over more rapidly; the level of raw material inventory could be reduced or the production period could be shortened. The operating cycle is only the *time-span* between production costs and cash returns; it says nothing in itself about the amount of working capital that will be needed over this period. In fact, less will be required at the beginning than at the end.

# DEBTOR MANAGEMENT

The typical company in the UK has a ratio of debtors to total assets in the region of 20–25 per cent. This represents a considerable investment of funds, and so the management of this asset can have a significant effect on the profit performance of a company. By international standards, the UK does not have a good record for the collection of debts. In the UK manufacturing sector it takes on average about 60 days for a company to collect the funds due from a debtor. In contrast, in the USA the average collection period for manufacturing industry is in the region of 40 days.

In order to reduce the debtor days to a more respectable figure companies will offer customers inducements, in the form of *cash discounts*. These discounts may well speed up collection but reduce the amount from each sale when collected.

Credit management involves balancing the benefits to be gained from extending credit to customers against the costs of doing so, and finding the optimum level of credit and discounts which will maximize the company's profits. It also involves such things as assessing the credit risk of customers wanting credit, collecting debts which are overdue, assessing what effect changing credit terms will have on the occurrence of bad debts, and setting individual credit limits for customers.

### The cost of credit
### (estimating the real cost of discounts)

The cost of offering a cash discount in order to generate better cash flow is sometimes overlooked. The savings made by the company from a lower debtor balance and shorter average collecting period should be compared with the cost of the discount to see if the reduced period of credit could be financed by alternative means – eg a bank overdraft.

## Example: simple interest approach

Claud Ltd normally offers its customers 50-day payment terms, but to improve its cash flow is considering a 2 per cent discount for payment within 10 days. Advise the company on the cost of this proposed action. Assume a 365-day year and an invoice for £100.

## Solution

$$\frac{2\%}{98\%} \times \frac{365}{50-10} = 18.6\%$$

The company would receive £98 on day 10 instead of £100 on day 50. Claud Ltd would then be able to invest the £98 for 40 days $(50-10)$.

The 18.6 per cent would then be compared with the company cost of capital to establish if this is an efficient method of financing the shorter credit period.

Note: a more accurate method can be used which deals with the compound interest effect.

The compound interest formula states that the value $V$ attained by a single sum $X$, after $n$ periods at $r$ per cent is:

$$V = X (1 + r)^n$$

Using this formula to quantify the cost of offering the cash discount:

$$100 = 98 (1 + r)^{365/40}$$

Rearranging the formula gives:

$$1 + r = 9.125\sqrt{\frac{100}{98}} \qquad 1 + r = 1.202$$

The cost of offering cash discounts is then 20.2 per cent.

*Credit control*

As stated above, to have good credit management you should assess the credit risk of your customer base. This would involve giving consideration to your credit control procedures. Detailed below are key elements of what you need to take into account in setting your *credit control policy*:

- The terms of trade, notably the period of credit to be granted, and any discounts to be allowed for early settlement. This will largely be determined by practice within the industry but there is usually some scope for differentiation – from competitors, and as between customers (the riskier prospects being put on a shorter-period, higher- discount arrangement). It is important to record all the terms agreed.
- On a customer-by-customer basis, it is necessary to assess creditworthiness and to establish limits in terms of amount and time. Late payment is seen as a major problem in UK industry – with large companies accused of pressurizing small ones – and various ideas have been put forward:
  - legislation to give suppliers a statutory right to interest on overdue debts;
  - disclosure in published accounts of credit taken;
  - a code of practice, including paying according to agreed terms;
  - inclusion of payment to agreed terms as a requisite for receiving a quality certificate.

Consideration should be given to assessing a customer's credit-worthiness, particularly for new customers. In addition, consider proceedings to review existing customers from time to time, especially if they request that their credit limit should be raised. Information about a customer's credit standing can be obtained from a variety of sources:

- *Bank references*   These tend to be fairly standardized in the UK, and so are not perhaps as helpful as they could be.
- *Trade references*   Suppliers already giving credit to the customer can give useful information about how good the customer is in paying bills on time.
- *Published information*   The customer's annual accounts and reports will give some idea of the general financial position of the company and its liquidity.
- *Credit agencies*   Agencies such as Dunn and Bradstreet publish general financial details of many companies, together with a credit rating. They will also produce a special report on a company if requested.
- *Company's own sales record*   For an existing customer, the sales ledger will show how prompt a payer the company is, although it cannot show how able the customer is to pay.

Assessing customers' creditworthiness can be expensive in terms of both time and money, and as with all credit management the costs and benefits have to be considered together. The more detailed and expensive investigations should be reserved for potentially important or especially risky customers. By tradition a company is supplied with the names of two trade creditors and the customer's banker when it is deciding whether or not to give credit. Much also comes down to a question of judgement.

### Chasing overdue accounts

- There need to be well-defined procedures for following up – allowing in the first instance for the possibility of a genuine query – keeping notes which can be referred to later. If the worst comes to the worst, there will be a need to understand the law relating to contracts, insolvency, winding up and liquidation. In practical terms, the danger of 'throwing good money after bad' needs to be considered.
- Ultimately, the choice may be between suing for the debt or instituting winding-up proceedings. One possibility is to

serve a statutory demand, as prescribed in the Insolvency Act 1986, after which the debtor has 21 days in which to apply for an injunction to prevent the presentation of a winding-up petition.

- For all practical purposes, the County Court is the focus for debt actions, although larger or more complex cases can go to the High Court. If successful, an action gives rise to a judgment debt which may trigger administration or liquidation.

*Assessing the effectiveness of credit control*

An outsider looking in, and wishing to assess the effectiveness of a credit control function, is generally limited to using static information and ratios, as illustrated in Table 6.4.

**Table 6.4** Assessing the effectiveness of credit control

|  | *Year 1* | *Year 2* |
|---|---|---|
| £ million: |  |  |
| (a) sales for the year | 100.0 | 120.0 |
| (b) debtors at the end of the year | 16.0 | 20.0 |
| Times per annum: |  |  |
| Asset velocity (a)/(b) | 6.3 | 6.0 |
| Days: |  |  |
| Average collection period 365(b)/(a) | 58.4 | 60.8 |

This would be interpreted as an apparent deterioration in performance, but such an approach inevitably ignores a number of possible explanations:

- changes in the pattern of sales across the year, eg more towards the end;
- changes in the mix of sales as between customers, eg more to those granted longer credit;
- changes in terms, eg less attractive discounts to some or all customers;

- different degrees of window-dressing, eg sales pulled forward from subsequent year.

Internally, of course, these problems do not arise, thanks to the availability of management information, including daily sales and receipts. As sales are entered into the ledger, for example, it is possible to identify when they should be paid, thus providing an appropriate yardstick against which to measure performance.

Enterprises which seek to apply the principles of value assurance to activities characterized as giving rise to 'indirect costs' could do worse than start with credit control. Value in this context is the cost of the next best alternative, eg handing over the job to the professional factors.

This amounts to regarding the function as a business unit. It is credited with its actual receipts having been debited with:

- the price at which the factor would buy the debts, eg 98 per cent of their face value;
- the cost of finance, say 0.03 per cent per day on the aggregate balance;
- the costs of administration etc.

If the net result is positive, the function is adding value to the enterprise.

### Factoring

One business process with which financial managers have a natural affinity, but which may nevertheless be contracted out, is the management of receivables. In many industries, the capital required to fund the granting of credit to customers represents a substantial proportion of the total and tends to vary directly with the level of activity: the greater the volume, the greater the investment in this particular component of current assets.

Rather than obtaining traditional finance (eg equity and overdrafts), some enterprises choose to define their businesses in such a way as to exclude this particular process. Effectively, they say that their business virtually ends at the point where goods are delivered. Specialist finance companies (again usually subsidiaries of banks) offer a factoring arrangement under which they:

- provide finance by advancing, say, 80 per cent of invoice value immediately, the remainder being settled when the client's customer settles the debt (but net of a charge for interest, typically 3 per cent per annum above base rate);
- take responsibility for the operation of the client's sales ledger, including assessment of creditworthiness and dealing with customers for an additional service charge, typically 2 per cent of turnover. They may even, for an additional fee, offer *non-recourse finance*, ie guarantee settlement even if they are not paid by the customer.

In order to do this economically, they have developed their expertise in credit control, in terms of market intelligence (including credit scoring), information management (sophisticated databases, processing and decision support systems) and the skills required for dealing with customers – especially those who are in no hurry to pay!

Alternatively, they may offer a confidential *invoice discounting facility* under which they provide the finance as above but do not get involved with the operation of the sales ledger or hence become known to the customers. This has, to date, been more popular than the overt factoring arrangement. It is cheaper, of course, and avoids creating a barrier between the business and its customers. It is less attractive to the providers of finance, however, being in the nature of supplying a commodity rather than adding value through expertise.

Though, as mentioned, these financiers are usually subsidiaries of banks, they like to distinguish their approach from that of their parents. They argue that the mainstream banks, when deciding on the extent to which they are prepared to lend, have traditionally looked backwards – to a company's past profits and tangible assets. This explains why they are reluctant to lend just when the company needs it, ie ahead of a growth phase. A sales-based package is a logical, flexible alternative. Having syphoned off the debtors in this way, however, the returns from a business are going to be more uncertain, making it difficult to raise more traditional forms of finance except at high interest rates. It is also worth noting that factoring is associated in many people's minds with financial difficulties ('the banks don't refer their best prospects to their factoring subsidiaries') or at best with small businesses, which may have an impact on the image of the business in the eyes of its creditors.

The volume of business (measured in terms of clients' turnover) in the UK is of the order of £15 billion per annum, the majority being invoice discounting. Surprisingly, the export content is less than 5 per cent. Letters of credit and forfeiting dominate the market, and there is also a considerable amount of barter. Apart from the factors and invoice discounters, it is worth noting some other players in the receivables industry:

- the specialist information providers, covering credit assessments, increasingly available electronically. This means that the sales function can have access, thereby reducing the potential for friction, ie taking an order only to find that 'finance' reject it on the grounds of credit risk;
- credit insurance, dominated in the UK by Trade Indemnity. Clients typically pay around 1 per cent of sales, depending on the industry into which they are selling and on their perceived credit control skills. It should be seen as complementary to, rather than a substitute for, in-house vigilance;
- debt collectors, often members of the legal profession, who take over responsibility for dealing with unpaid bills – sometimes on commission, otherwise for a fee.

These various services are mutually supportive, and there have been signs of convergence, ie of providers who offer a menu from which businesses can pick. The financial implications of a factoring agreement may need to be evaluated with regard to alternative financing methods.

*Example*

B plc has been set up for the purpose of importing commodities which will be sold to a small number of reliable customers. Sales invoicing is forecast at £300,000 per month. The average credit period for this type of business is two and a half months.

The company is considering factoring its accounts receivable under a full factoring agreement without recourse. Under the agreement the factor will charge a fee of 2.5 per cent on total invoicing. He will give an advance of 85 per cent of invoiced amounts at an interest rate of 13 per cent per annum. The agreement should enable B plc to avoid spending £95,000 on administration costs.

*Required*

1. calculate the annual net cost of factoring and
2. consider the financial benefits of such an agreement, having regard to current interest rate on bank overdrafts of 12.5 per cent.

*Solution*

1.
Annual sales: £300,000 × 12                          £3,600,000

| Annual net cost of factoring | [£] |
|---|---|
| Fee: 2.5% of £3,600,000 | 90,000 |
| Annual interest* (85% × 2.5/12 × 3.6m × 13%) | 82,875 |
| Total annual cost | 172,875 |
| Less: administration costs | 95,000 |
| Net cost | 77,875 |

* Assuming the agreement is based on existing invoices and does not phase in.

2.  The borrowing of £637,500 ie (2.5/12 × 3.6m × 85%) from the bank would cost £79,687.50). Therefore, factoring offers a saving of around £2,000 as well as providing certain advantages:

- *Flexibility* As sales increase with the corresponding demand for finance, so finance from this source increases.
- *Security* It allows the firm to pledge other assets as security for the finance.
- *Last resort* It may be the most cost-effective lender to a firm which has no assets to offer as security.
- *Responsibility* Relieves management of the responsibility for the sales ledger and can probably perform credit-checking better than the firm. Management must balance the disruption from cutting back its administrative costs with the financial and other advantages of factoring. Before reaching a decision, management should consider the possibility that the financial advantages may change and that re-establishing a sales ledger function may be costly.

## STOCK MANAGEMENT

Stocks, like debtors, involve the commitment of a large amount of a firm's resources. Their efficient management is of great concern to the financial manager. Stocks include raw materials, bought-in parts, finished goods awaiting sale and also work in progress, although the latter element will not be discussed here. Stocks should not be viewed as an idle asset; rather, they are an essential part of a firm's investment and operations. The optimum holding of stocks will maximize the benefits less costs involved.

Holding higher levels of finished goods stock will enable the company to be more flexible in supplying customers. More customers would receive immediate delivery rather than waiting for new items to be produced and they might obtain a greater choice of types of product. There would be a smaller chance of sales being disrupted through interruptions in production. These benefits would have to be balanced against the storage costs incurred, the capital costs of financing the stock and the cost of stock becoming obsolete.

The EOQ (economic order quality) model provides a method of calculating an optimum batch or order which minimizes these costs.

$$EOQ = \sqrt{\frac{2C_0 D}{C_h}}$$

where

$C_0$ = cost of making an order
$D$ = annual demand
$C_h$ = holding cost per unit of stock for one year

This model assumes that:

- demand is constant;
- lead time is constant;
- purchase costs per unit are constant.

## *Example*

The demand for an item of stock is 50,000 units per annum. It costs £25 to place an order and 60p to hold 1 unit for a year.

## *Required*

Identify the order size to minimize stock costs and the number of orders placed each year.

## *Solution*

$$EOQ = \sqrt{\frac{2C_0 D}{C_h}} = \sqrt{\frac{2 \times 25 \times 50,000}{0.6}} = 2,041 \text{ units}$$

The number of orders placed each year is 50,000/2,041 = 24.5, ie 25.

## *Just in time (JIT) purchasing*

Developed by the Japanese, it is claimed that the implementation of JIT systems has been one of the major factors contributing to their success. It involves a continuous commitment to the pursuit of excellence in all phases of manufacturing. Its aims are to produce the required items of the required quality in the required quantity at the required time.

There are two aspects to JIT; JIT purchasing, and JIT production. With JIT purchasing it means that materials or components are received from the supplier just in time to use them. They are in effect delivered to the factory floor.

The objectives of JIT purchasing may be stated as:

- raw material stock reduction;
- frequent deliveries with smaller orders from a smaller number of suppliers;
- long-term contracts with suppliers;
- quality assurance, with the supplier becoming responsible for the inspection of goods supplied.

The objectives of JIT production are to obtain low-cost, high-quality, on-time production, to order, by minimizing stock levels between successive processes and, therefore, minimizing idle equipment, facilities and workers.

The introduction of JIT may bring the following benefits:

- reduced inventory;
- savings in storage space required;
- increased customer satisfaction – elimination of waste will lead to a better-quality product;
- weaknesses and problems may be identified – problems such as bottlenecks, supplier reliability, and inadequate documentation may be revealed;
- flexibility and the ability to supply small batches.

JIT will not, however, be appropriate in all situations. A full work study will be required to look at the production methods. A large amount of capital is needed to operate a JIT system, and flexibility is lost due to the nature of the contracts with suppliers.

## CREDITOR MANAGEMENT

Trade credit is normally viewed as being a free source of finance. The policy adopted regarding trade creditors often then tends to be to maximize this resource, paying suppliers as late as possible. This policy may lead to difficulties in obtaining credit terms with new suppliers. It may also lead to cash-flow problems for key suppliers, which could adversely affect the viability of both organizations. Creditor management will broadly reflect debtor management, as one organization's debtor will be another organization's creditor.

## CASH MANAGEMENT

The management of cash resources holds a central position in the area of short-term financing decisions. Results of investment decisions are estimated in cash terms and the value of a company to shareholders lies in its ability to add to their command over resources over time, which means to add to shareholders' command over cash.

Holding cash carries with it a cost – the *opportunity cost* of the profits which could be made if the cash was either used in the company or invested elsewhere. Therefore, a company has to balance the advantages of liquidity against profitability: cash should be held until the marginal value of the liquidity it gives is equal to the value of the interest lost.

Cash management is, therefore, concerned with optimizing the amount of cash available to the company, and maximizing the interest on any spare funds not required immediately by the company.

## The time value of money

A recurring theme of financial management is the time value of money – or the money value of time, depending on your point of view. The need to offer the prospect of an adequate return is an important element in the setting of business objectives. That need is quantified as 'the cost of capital' for use as a criterion against which to make decisions and monitor their implementation.

It needs to be remembered, however, that there is no one generally applicable, constant price of money. Interest rates vary, according to the length of time of the investment, as portrayed in the familiar yield curve, and the yield curve itself varies over time. Interest rates are different according to whether you are lending to, or borrowing from, the banking system, and according to the flexibility of the arrangement, eg how much notice is required to move funds into or out of an account.

Other things being equal, in what amounts to a reflection of their expected costs, the banks pay higher interest on accounts subject to longer notices of withdrawal than they do on current accounts and charge higher interest on fluctuating overdrafts than they do on term loans.

A key task for the treasury function in any enterprise, therefore, is the management of the various accounts. Money is switched between them, so as to minimize aggregate costs (or maximize net income, as the case may be), recognizing both transaction costs and interest rate differentials.

Early theories in this area (generally credited to W J Baumol in the early 1950s) borrowed from the techniques which had been developed for controlling stocks. Assume, for example, that:

- outgoings are £300,000 per annum, spread evenly throughout the year;
- money on deposit earns 10 per cent per annum more than money in a current account;
- switching costs £20 per transaction.

According to Baumol, the optimum amount to be transferred (in £) each time is stated as:

$$\sqrt{\frac{2 \times \text{transaction costs} \times \text{outgoings}}{\text{deposit rate}}}$$

that is:

$$\sqrt{\frac{2 \times 20 \times 300,000}{0.1}}$$

ie approximately £11,000. At this point, the number of transactions would be around 27 per annum, the average balance in the short-notice account would be £5,500, for an aggregate cost of £540 + £550, ie £1,090 per annum.

Such a model was a gross oversimplification, of course, but did draw attention to the directional impact of the various factors, eg were the interest rate differential to be increased, then the size of the optimum transfer would be reduced.

One of the most serious weaknesses was seen to be the assumption that the net cash outflow from the short-notice account was steady and, therefore, predictable. In the real world there are bound to be fluctuations, the exact timing of which may be difficult to predict. So, in the late 1950s, a more elaborate approach was developed, M H Miller and D Orr being credited with its origination.

Their idea was to transfer money into or out of the account to return the balance to a predetermined 'normal point' whenever the actual balance went outside a lower or upper limit (respectively, assuming the account is always in credit). The lower limit would be set by management, and the upper limit and return points by way of formulae which assume that cash inflows and outflows are random, their dispersion usually being assumed to repeat a pattern exhibited in the past. For the record, the formulae are:

- Spread between upper and lower limits =

$$3 \times \left( \frac{\frac{3}{4} \times \text{transaction cost} \times \text{variance of cash flows}}{\text{interest rate}} \right)^{1/3}$$

- Return point = lower limit plus one-third of spread.

Assume, for example, that:

- a lower control limit of £1,000 is decided upon;
- the interest rate is 0.025 per cent per day;
- the standard deviation of the daily cash flows has been measured as £500, ie a variance of £250,000;
- switching costs £20 per transaction.

Then the spread would be

$$3 \times \left( \frac{\frac{3}{4} \times £20 \times £250,000}{0.00025} \right)^{1/3}$$

ie approximately £7,400. Hence the upper limit would be £8,400 and the return point £3,467.

Again, the directional pointers provide useful reminders, eg if the variability of cash flows increases, so does the spread. Variations on the theme can be developed to take account of seasonality, numerous different accounts, the lead time between breaking the limit and cash actually being transferred, etc, but these are likely to be of only specialist appeal.

More to the point is the recognition that cash flows are not completely random, are not totally unpredictable and are not independently variable. Treasurers will be forewarned of many of the payments to be made, eg wages, dividends and tax. Also, they will have some flexibility as regards the timing of many others, eg to hold a payment to a creditor until after receipt from a debtor. Consequently, as in so many fields, decisions are rarely made on the basis of models which require you to believe that cash flows behave like a game of chance, constrained by a pattern derived from an analysis of the facts of the past.

Rather, they are made on the basis of a synthesis of judgements about the future. Spreadsheets provide a useful form in which to prepare and express these, and offer the facility of asking the 'what if?' type of question.

## *New technology and payment systems*

The development of electronic funds transfer systems has considerably improved the speed with which cash payments can be made between companies, and between companies and their customers or employees. The following are examples:

- CHAPS (Clearing House Automated Payment System) provides same day settlements for amounts of £10,000 or more between banks which are members of the clearing system.
- BACS (Bankers Automated Clearance Services) is a financial transfer system applying to accounts in UK banks, and is most concerned with the processing of payrolls and with transactions involving standing orders and direct debits. An advantage is that the payer is not debited until the day on which the payee is credited. However, the method can be expensive and recent appraisals have highlighted that it is only cost-effective for regular and low-value payments. Nevertheless, it is widely used for payroll processing.
- SWIFT (Society for Worldwide Interbank Financial Telecommunications) is a network which provides for the rapid transmission of international remittances between participant banks on a worldwide basis. It is possible for organizations other than banks to become eligible users, such as recognized exchanges, central clearers and securities houses.
- VISA (VISA International) now permits participant banks to transmit credits as well as debits to each other through its data network; it provides low-value cross-border payment services for individuals and small businesses in respect of a number of European countries.

## MANAGING CASH SURPLUSES

Cash surpluses arise for many reasons and last for varying time periods. In principle, where there is no foreseeable use for the surpluses the cash should be returned to shareholders, or used to repay debt. Usually, though, cash will be retained to protect against unexpected losses or to fund unexpected investment opportunities.

The treasurer will need to consider opportunities for short-term investment in order to put any cash surpluses to work. The following considerations should be made in assessing how to invest short-term cash surpluses:

- length of time for which the funds are available;
- amount of funds available;
- return offered on the investment in relation to the amount involved;
- risks associated with calling in the investment early (eg the need to give three months' notice to obtain the interest);
- ease of realization.

The aim for the treasurer is to maximize the post-tax return from the investment, but also to minimize the risk to the original capital invested. Examples of short-term investment opportunities that the treasurer may consider include:

- *Treasury bills* Issued by the Bank of England and guaranteed by the UK government. No interest is paid as such, but they are issued at a discount and redeemed at par after 91 days. At any time the bills can be sold on the discount market.
- *Bank deposits* A wide range of financial instruments are available from banks, but the more established investment opportunities are:
  - term deposits where, for a fixed period (usually from one month to six years) a fixed rate is given. For shorter

periods (typically up to three months) the interest may be at a variable rate based on money market rates;

- certificates of deposit, issued by the banks at a fixed interest rate for a fixed term (usually between three months and five years) but which can be realized on the discount market at any time.

- *Money market accounts* Most major financial institutions offer schemes for investment in the money market at variable rates of interest.

It is unlikely that short-term cash surpluses will be invested in equities because of the risks associated with achieving a return over a short period.

## *OVERDRAFTS*

One of the most important external sources of short-term finance, particularly for small firms, is the overdraft. Features that make overdraft finance popular are:

- *Flexibility* The bank will agree to a maximum overdraft limit, or facility. The borrower may not require the full facility immediately, but may draw funds up to the limit as and when required.
- *Minimal documentation* Legal documentation is fairly minimal when arranging an overdraft. Key elements of the documentation will be to state the maximum overdraft limit, the interest rate payable, and the security required.
- Interest is only paid on the amount borrowed, rather than on the full facility.

Drawbacks of overdraft finance are that it is, strictly speaking, repayable on demand, which means that the facility could be withdrawn at any time. Companies with few assets to offer as security will find it difficult to arrange further overdraft finance. The interest rate charged by the bank will vary depending on the perceived credit risk of the borrower.

## SUMMARY

In this chapter we have seen that working capital policy is concerned with two main areas: the investment in working capital items and how those working capital items should be financed. It is important for the treasury manager to be aware of the opportunity costs arising from inadequate control of working capital, and we have considered a range of techniques that may be used to manage debtors, stocks, creditors and cash.

Factoring and invoice discounting have been considered in this chapter as techniques for the management of receivables, but they could equally have been considered in Chapter 3 as useful alternative methods of raising finance, particularly for small- and medium-sized businesses.

# 7

# Management of Interest Rate Risk

Large companies, particularly multinationals, often rely heavily on the financial markets for finance. Interest and exchange rates change continually, often by significant amounts, which makes these markets extremely volatile. One of the treasurer's responsibilities is to manage an organization's exposure to interest and currency risks.

In this chapter we begin by identifying some of the main influences on interest rates before looking at some of the techniques available for hedging interest rate risk.

## *INTEREST RATE RISK*

Businesses wish to reduce their exposure to risk in all its forms and much has been written on this topic, ranging from the identification of different elements of risk (interest rate, foreign exchange, political), through to its quantification (portfolio theory and capital asset pricing model). There remain, however, large areas of uncertainty.

The sources of uncertainty cover a wide area but it is worth noting that economic and political trends are major contributory factors. In particular, in the 1980s the move away from using interest rates to manage demand (Keynesian economics) to their use in controlling the money supply led to increased volatility around the world, particularly in the UK and the USA, and this has a knock-on effect with exchange rates, as international capital moves to countries with increasing interest rates boosting the exchange rate. The unification of Germany produced similar problems within the EC, as Germany used high interest rates to attempt to control the expansion of its money supply caused by the exchange rate set between the East and West currencies. This led to high rates across Europe as countries tried to maintain their exchange rates within the ERM. The turmoil of autumn 1992 may have been bad for politicians but it reintroduced exchange risk to financial managers based in the UK and trading within the EC.

Currency risk and the methods for dealing with it are considered in Chapters 8, 9 and 10. *Interest rate risk* deals with the possibility of loss arising from a change in the level of interest rates.

## *Example*

As both a borrower and an investor of funds, a company is exposed to variations in the interest rate. For example, in Figure 7.1, if a medium-term loan is taken out at a rate of, say, 15 per cent (variable), and interest rates are falling, the changing interest rates will work to the advantage of the company. Conversely, if interest rates were rising, or if the loan was fixed rate, the change would be detrimental to the company. One important aspect of the treasury function is management of debt in such a way as to reduce the company's exposure to risk resulting from interest rate movements.

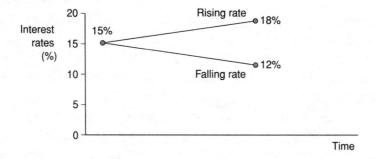

**Figure 7.1** Interest rate exposure

## *Term structure of interest rates*

One of the primary considerations in evaluating debt is the likely movement in interest rates. This will affect the relative costs of long- and short-term debt, as well as increasing or decreasing the preference for fixed interest rates. In practice, long-term rates will normally be higher than short-term rates, owing to the additional risk borne by the lender. Hence an interest premium is required to attract investors to longer-term securities.

This effect may be magnified or reversed by investors' expectations of future rates, an anticipated rate rise producing higher longer-term rates. This difference between long- and short-term rates is known as term structure.

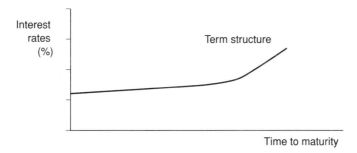

**Figure 7.2** Term structure

Figure 7.2 shows an upward-sloping term structure (although it may be flat or downward sloping), showing long-term rates to be higher than those available in the short term. In extreme cases, this may justify a company borrowing, using short-dated stock which is replaced regularly, although the level of transaction costs makes this unlikely.

### *Factors that influence term structure*

In general terms, an increasing term structure results from two factors: (1) increased risk of longer debt; and (2) anticipated general interest rate rises. More detailed analysis is required, however.

Below are listed formal theories as to why interest rates increase with time.

## Expectations theory

This states that the forward interest rate is due solely to expectations of interest rate movements. If an individual wishes to borrow for two years, two obvious possibilities present themselves: borrow for two years at an agreed rate; or borrow for one year and refinance for the second year (ie pay off the first loan by taking out a second).

In option (1), the interest paid on the loan will be based on the current interest rate and the forward rate for one year; and in option (2) the individual will consider the current interest rate and the expected interest rate for year two. Thus the choice between the options hinges on whether the forward rate for year two is higher or lower than the expected rate.

From the lender's point of view, if the expected rate was higher they would only lend short, preferring to renegotiate at the end of one year and take advantage of the anticipated rate rise. A similar argument could be made if the expected rate was lower than the forward rate. Thus, for long- and short-dated debt to coexist, expected future rates and forward rates must be equal. Thus the term structure of interest rates is due purely to investor expectations.

## Liquidity preference theory

The problem with the expectations theory is that it ignores risk – if the expected rate for year two is the same as the forward rate then an individual needing to borrow for two years would choose a two-year loan since this eliminates the uncertainty of the actual interest rate to be paid in year two. Thus, borrowers will aim to borrow for the period for which they need funds. If lenders wish only to lend for one year there will be a shortage of long funds and an excess of short funds. This will lead to a premium on forward rates, ie lenders will get a bonus for lending for two years and borrowers will have to pay extra if they insist on a two-year loan. In this case the term structure of interest rates would again be upward-sloping but now it would be due to the liquidity preference of lenders and borrowers.

*Market segmentation*

It has been argued that demand for capital funds in practice can be segmented, particularly on a time basis. Thus, for example, companies tend to finance stocks with short-term funds and equipment with long-term funds. This leads to different factors affecting long- and short-term rates and a lack of a clear trend in the yield curve, characterized by irregularities such as humps and dips.

## INTEREST RATE RISK MANAGEMENT

The traditional method of managing interest rate risk has been fixed-rate borrowing in the form of loans. It is simple, and companies know how much they will need each year to service the debt. However, it is not always possible to obtain a loan at the rates, or for the amounts, required.

An enterprise may wish to take precautions against interest rates moving up or down in the future, or may wish to change the existing structure of its funding or deposits, for instance from a fixed rate of interest to a floating rate. With the development of the financial markets and, in particular, the financial futures markets, a number of instruments have arisen which allow the treasurer to hedge interest rate risk.

### Interest rate swaps

An interest rate swap is an exchange of interest rate commitments, such that a fixed-rate commitment is exchanged for a floating-rate commitment. The parties to a swap retain their obligations to the original lenders, which means that the swap parties must accept counterparty risk.

## Example

Lockwood plc has a high credit rating. It can borrow at a fixed rate of 10 per cent or at a variable interest rate of LIBOR + 0.3 per cent. It would like to borrow at a variable rate.

Thomas plc has a lower credit rating. It can borrow at a fixed rate of 11 per cent or at a variable rate of LIBOR + 0.5 per cent. It would like to borrow at a fixed rate.

Using the principle of comparative advantage, both parties could benefit from a swap arrangement, whereby:

- Lockwood plc borrows at a fixed rate of 10 per cent;
- Thomas plc borrows at a variable rate of LIBOR + 0.5 per cent;
- the parties agree a rate for swapping their interest commitments with, perhaps: Thomas plc paying a fixed rate of 10.1 per cent to Lockwood plc, and Lockwood plc paying a variable rate of LIBOR to Thomas plc.

The outcome would be:

*Lockwood plc*

| | |
|---|---|
| Borrows at | 10% |
| Receives from Thomas plc | (10.1%) |
| Pays to Thomas plc | LIBOR |
| Net interest cost | LIBOR – 0.1% |

(a saving of 0.4%)

*Thomas plc*

| | |
|---|---|
| Borrows at | LIBOR + 0.5% |
| Receives from Lockwood plc | (LIBOR) |
| Pays to Lockwood plc | 10.1% |
| Net interest cost | 10.6% |

(a saving of 0.4%)

In this example, both companies benefit from lower interest costs. The example is shown in diagrammatical form in Figure 7.3.

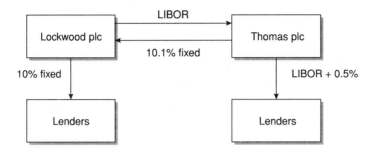

**Figure 7.3** Interest rate swaps

Interest rate swaps are used for purposes other than obtaining a cheaper financing rate. They could, for example, be used to change future cash flows, or to enhance returns.

Interest rate swaps are off balance sheet items, as the principal amount of the contract is not paid, and it is just an agreement to swap future cash flows. However, the existence of the swap should be mentioned in the notes to the financial statements. The interest payments and receipts should be accrued over the life of the swap on a straight line basis. Financial institutions which actively trade swaps revalue their positions to the current market value.

### *Forward-rate agreements*

A forward-rate agreement (FRA) is an agreement whereby an enterprise can lock in an interest rate today for a period of time starting in the future. On the future date the two counterparties in the FRA settle up and, depending on which way rates go, one will pay an amount of money to the other representing the difference between the FRA rate and the actual rate.

### *Example*

Thompson plc has a £1 million loan outstanding, on which the interest rate is reset every six months for the following six months, and the interest is payable at the end of that six-month period.

The next six-monthly reset period may now be just three months' away, but the treasurer of Thompson plc thinks that interest rates are likely to rise between now and then. Current six-month rates are 8 per cent and the treasurer can get a rate of 8.1 per cent for a six-month FRA starting in three months' time. By transacting an FRA the treasurer can lock in a rate today of 8.1 per cent. If interest rates rise as expected to, say, 9 per cent Thompson plc has reduced its interest charge as it will pay the current 9 per cent rate on its loan but will receive from the FRA counterparty the difference between 9 per cent and 8.1 per cent.

If, however, rates drop to 7 per cent, Thompson plc will still end up paying an effective rate of 8.1 per cent because, although the interest rate on the loan is lower, the company will pay the FRA counterparty the difference between the 7 per cent and 8.1 per cent.

*If rates are 9 per cent in three months' time:*

|  | £ |
|---|---|
| Interest payable on the loan 9% × £1m × 6/12 | 45,000 |
| Amount receivable on FRA (9% – 8.1%) × £1m × 6/12 | (4,500) |
| Net amount | 40,500 |

The £40,500 is the net amount payable, giving an effective rate of 8.1 per cent.

*If rates are 7 per cent in three months' time:*

|  | £ |
|---|---|
| Interest payable on the loan 7% × £1m × 6/12 | 35,000 |
| Amount payable on FRA (8.1% – 7%) × £1m × 6/12 | 5,500 |
| Net amount | 40,500 |

The £40,500 is the net amount payable, again giving an effective rate of 8.1 per cent.

## *Interest rate futures*

Futures are standardized traded forms of FRAs, and the above FRA example could also have been used for an interest rate future. Table 7.1 below summarizes some of the differences between an FRA and a future. FRAs are normally transacted with banks and other financial institutions, and because of this they are tailor-made to suit the dates and amounts that each individual company requires. However, interest rate futures are exchange-traded and each contract is for a pre-specified amount and date. In the UK, interest rate futures are traded on the London International Financial Futures and Options Exchange (LIFFE).

If a company does not need a specific amount or set dates then futures are useful. For most organizations, however, they are not so convenient. There are also administrative problems with daily margin payments on futures contracts which many organizations find burdensome. However, futures contracts are very liquid – it is easy to liquidate a contract. This is not so common with FRAs. In the above FRA example the treasurer could not have sold on his FRA but would have needed to take out a second FRA with the reverse effect of the first. With a future it is a very easy matter just to sell the future back. In practice many organizations use FRAs, relatively few use futures.

**Table 7.1** FRAs and futures compared

|  | *FRAs* | *Futures* |
|---|---|---|
| Amount | Any amount | Only standard round sum amounts |
| Dates | Any dates | Only pre-specified dates – normally March, June, September and December |
| Payments | One only on settlement date | Initial and thereafter daily variation margin payments |
| Delivery | As per contract | Most are liquidated before maturity |
| Credit | With the counter-party | Very limited risk because of margin payments and the exchange acts as buyer and seller of every contract |
| Market | Over-the-counter | Exchange traded |

The pricing of interest rate futures is based on taking the interest rate away from 100. Thus if the interest rate was 7 per cent then the futures price would be 100 – 7, ie 93. If the interest rate were 12 per cent the futures price would be 100 – 12, ie 88. Futures contracts can be bought or sold. If the company were hedging against interest rates rising, for instance, where interest payments were due, a futures contract would be sold. Suppose that the interest rate was 7 per cent and thus the futures price was 93. The company could sell the futures contract at 93. If rates then moved up to 8 per cent the futures price would be 92. The company would lose out on the loan interest as it would now have to pay 8 per cent instead of 7 per cent. However, the company would profit on the futures contract, by 93 – 92, ie 1 per cent, which would offset the increase in loan interest. This is because the company originally sold the futures contract at a price of 93 when rates were 7 per cent and purchased later when rates had moved up to 8 per cent and the futures price was 92. If a company wished to hedge against interest rates decreasing, for instance, if it was to deposit money, then it would buy the contract initially, and then sell the contract at a later date. Both FRAs and futures 'lock' in a price today for a transaction which will occur at some time in the future.

### Interest rate options

An option is the right, but not the obligation, to carry out a transaction at a price set today, at some time in the future. Swaps, FRAs and futures are all contracts which two parties agree to transact and which must be carried out even if circumstances change. An option, however, gives the buyer the choice of whether to transact or not. A company would generally buy an option from an option seller or option writer. An option is a form of insurance, and as such a premium is paid at the time the option is taken out, for the period of the option. In the FRA example above, Thompson plc paid a net amount of £40,500 no matter what happened to interest rates.

Let us suppose that, instead of transacting the FRA above, an option was bought, entitling the buyer of the option to pay the same interest rate of 8.1 per cent. This is known as the strike price. The period of the option is for three months, which is when the renewal period for the loan starts. Suppose that the option premium paid today is £1,000. In three months' time we could have the same scenarios.

*If rates are 9 per cent in three months' time:*

|  | £ |
|---|---|
| Interest payable on the loan 9% × £1m × 6/12 | 45,000 |
| Exercise the option at a strike price of 8.1%, receive | (4,500) |
| Plus premium paid | 1,000 |
| Net amount | 41,500 |

*If rates are 7 per cent in three months' time:*

|  | £ |
|---|---|
| Interest payable on the loan 7% × £1m × 6/12 | 35,000 |
| Plus premium paid | 1,000 |
| Net amount | 36,000 |

Thus, if interest rates are 9 per cent in three months' time, Thompson plc will pay a net amount of £41,500 in interest over the six-month period, which is more than with the FRA because of the option premium. However, if rates fall to 7 per cent, only £36,000 will be paid, as the company does not need to exercise the option. An option is, therefore, not quite so favourable when rates go as expected, but much better when rates move in the opposite direction. Thus, with an option a company can take advantage of favourable interest rate movements.

Interest rate options can be purchased from banks, while standardized interest rate options are traded on LIFFE. A number of companies now also use 'swaptions', which are options on transacting a swap at a future date, and some companies may find these useful.

*Caps, floors and collars*

An interest rate cap is an option which sets a maximum interest rate on future borrowings for an agreed length of time. A floor is an option that sets a minimum interest rate. A collar arises when a borrower buys an interest rate cap and at the same time sells an interest rate floor. The premium received from selling the floor will reduce the cost of the premium paid for the cap. This is illustrated in Figure 7.4.

*Example*

Tandijono plc can currently borrow at 11 per cent, but is concerned that interest rates may rise in the near future to 14 per cent or more. In this situation the company could buy an interest rate cap from a bank which will fix the maximum rate for borrowing. The bank will reimburse the company if market interest rates rise above the cap rate.

As part of the arrangement, the company may also agree that it will pay a floor rate of, say, 10 per cent. The bank will pay a premium to the company for agreeing to this floor rate.

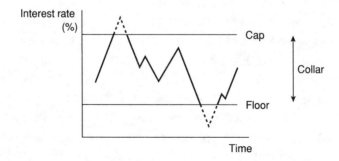

**Figure 7.4** Caps, floors and collars

## *SUMMARY*

Interest rate risk is a problem faced by all companies with gearing. Given the past volatility of interest rates, an awareness of the risks of interest rate movements is important. In this chapter we have considered some of the influences on interest rate movement, and identified a range of techniques that may be used to reduce exposure to interest rate risk, such as interest rate swaps, forward-rate agreements, futures and options.

# 8

# Currency Risks

As companies take a more global perspective to their trading activities, investing overseas and the financing of such operations will be given greater consideration. We begin this chapter by considering the methods available to an organization wishing to finance an overseas operation. We then introduce some foreign exchange terminology which will also be used in Chapters 9 and 10.

It is important for the treasury manager to be aware of the risks involved, and the various components of currency risk are considered. Currency risk may also be faced even if an enterprise has no overseas operations, or transactions with a currency component, and this is also considered in this chapter.

## FINANCING OVERSEAS OPERATIONS – A GLOBAL STRATEGY

In times past a business would, in its early days, tend to be concentrated in one geographical area, and in the regulated environment which used to pertain, even quite large companies would define themselves in national terms, and raise capital and invest in facilities where their market was. If asked about competition, they would naturally think of other enterprises based in the same country.

But that was then. Now, it is feasible – and in some instances vital – for enterprises to *raise capital* in one country, *invest it in another*, and produce goods which are to be marketed in a third. Moreover, they need to think about competition on a worldwide basis. As a result of this, companies have developed global strategies, perhaps to exploit new markets or secure supplies of raw materials that are essential for its UK or other worldwide operations. The £739 million purchase of Pedro Domecq (a Spanish sherry and brandy producer) in 1995 by the then named Allied-Lyons was a prime example of a company following a strategic global growth policy. In the long term they are hoping to form a company with sufficient capacity to sell a range of drinks in the biggest consumer market in the world, China.

The financing of these ventures is obviously of key importance if the risks outlined below are to be minimized. A number of different methods can be used to finance companies overseas.

### *Retained earnings*

The subsidiary could rely upon its own internally generated funds. This would avoid many of the problems of financing overseas, but is unlikely to result in the necessary level of expansion to meet high-growth objectives, and is obviously not suitable for new overseas ventures.

### *Finance from the UK*

Funds can be raised by the parent company within the UK and transferred overseas to subsidiary companies by way of a combination of equity and loans.

The main advantage of this method is that the company will probably be familiar with the UK capital markets and, therefore, be capable of raising finance quickly and cost-effectively. However, if exchange controls exist this method can become difficult and expensive.

Another disadvantage of using sterling-denominated finance for an overseas asset is that it will in no way reduce foreign exchange risk through matching (this is discussed in Chapter 9). The company will also be more exposed to political risks. If the investment is lost, perhaps through a war or expropriation by a foreign government, the UK liability will still remain intact. Also, if the overseas investment is a subsidiary company, then if the subsidiary fails the holding company is left with the liability in the same way.

### Finance in the overseas country

The main advantage of this method is that it will result in reductions in risk. Foreign exchange risk will be reduced since any losses in the value of the overseas asset will be offset by gains on the liability and vice versa. The complete elimination of risk is, however, unlikely since it would require the exact matching of cash flows on the asset and liability. Political risk can also be reduced since, if the investment is lost, the liability will be eliminated as well.

Difficulties may be experienced with this method of finance if the country concerned does not have a well-developed capital market. On the other hand, financing in the overseas country can make such investments more acceptable to that country since it is then seen that not all of the profits made are sent abroad. Alternatively, it could also be argued that financing overseas limits the methods by which profits from the overseas investment can be repatriated – heavy reliance being placed upon the payment of dividends. When finance is raised in the UK it may be easier to get money out of the country as a combination of dividends, interest, management charges, etc.

Most governments take steps to encourage overseas investors since they are beneficial to that country's economy, creating employment and wealth. Such encouragement often takes the form of grants, subsidies and cheap or guaranteed finance. These incentives should be taken into account when considering overseas investments and their financing.

### Financing from other capital markets

Finance can today be raised from a variety of capital markets. A multinational company based in the UK could quite easily raise finance in Germany via a subsidiary in that country and use the money to finance an investment in a different country or even in the UK. One possible incentive in raising money in other countries is that interest rates may be substantially lower than in the UK or in the country where an investment is intended. However, if the interest cost is lower then it is likely that the currency borrowed is strong and will, therefore, appreciate with respect to sterling and other currencies. The expected exchange loss on the borrowings would, therefore, offset any benefit through a lower interest rate.

### *Foreign exchange terminology*

#### *Spot rate*

This is the current exchange rate quoted by a bank for transactions which are due for immediate or very imminent completion. For example, a bank might quote a rate for US$ of:

$/£
1.6495 – 1.6500

The first figure quoted ($1.6495:£1) is the rate at which the bank will sell $ for £ today. The second figure quoted ($1.6500:£1) is the rate at which the bank will buy $ for £ today. Two rates are quoted because the bank will make its profit by buying currency at one rate and selling it at another.

#### *Forward rate*

This is the rate which is quoted today for transactions that will be completed on a specified future date. The forward rate is calculated arithmetically using the interest rate parity relationship which is discussed in Chapter 9. A bank might quote a one-month forward rate for US$ of:

$/£
1.6476 – 1.6480

Here a customer could agree to sell US$ to the bank in one month's time at an exchange rate of $1.6480:£1, or agree to buy US$ from the bank at rate of $1.6476:£1. Forward rates are sometimes expressed as an adjustment to the spot rate in the following way:

(a) *Discount* This is added to the spot rate to arrive at the forward rate. This implies that the forward rate is cheaper than the spot rate.

(b) *Premium* This is subtracted from the spot rate to arrive at the forward rate. This implies that the forward rate for a currency is more expensive than the spot rate.

## *Example*

A bank is currently quoting the following rates for sterling spot and forward:

|  | $/£ |  |
|---|---|---|
| Spot | 1.3915 – 1.3925 | |
| 1 month forward | 1.00 | – 0.90c pm |
| 2 months' forward | 1.60 | – 1.50c pm |
| 3 months' forward | 2.10 | – 2.00c pm |

(a) The bank will buy spot dollars at a rate of $1.3925:£1
(b) The bank will buy dollars one month forward at a rate of $1.3835:£1

| ie spot rate | 1.3925 |
|---|---|
| less premium | 0.0090 |
| | 1.3835 |

(c) The bank will sell dollars two months' forward at a rate of $1.3755:£1

| ie spot rate | 1.3915 |
|---|---|
| less premium | 0.0160 |
| | 1.3755 |

(d) The bank will buy dollars three months' forward at a rate of $1.3725:£1

| ie spot rate | 1.3925 |
|---|---|
| less premium | 0.0200 |
| | 1.3725 |

## OVERSEAS RISK

The ability of companies to successfully raise capital overseas, and thus expand their worldwide operations, has brought increased uncertainty, of course. Not only do we have to be alert to our international competitors' technological, marketing and managerial advances, but we have to think about the risks associated with currency volatility, interest rate changes and the political/social/economic climate. Most observers distinguish between two types of risk which affect the value of the entity as a whole (transactional and economic) and one which doesn't (translational). We look at them in that order.

## TRANSACTION RISKS

Foreign exchange transactions for immediate effect (or to be precise, unless special arrangements are made, for completion in a couple of days) are known as 'spot' transactions, conducted at the 'spot' rate. In the UK, exchange rates are quoted as selling price/buying price expressed in terms of currency per pound, eg £1 = $1.4980/90. Thus the bank would give you $1.4980 for each of your pounds or give you £1 for every 1.4990 of your dollars. The difference of one-tenth of a cent is the dealer's margin. Some markets are very large but others are so small that it is better to go through two stages, eg convert yen into deutschmarks, then convert the deutschmarks into sterling.

In these days of deregulation the rates vary considerably over time, and this is the source of various risks. Transaction risks are essentially those associated with the delays between transactions and settlements. They occur at the operational level of control, having a measurable effect on results, but need to be thoroughly understood before moving on to the higher levels. By way of illustration, we can think in terms of a business based in the UK which:

- on 1 November, took delivery of some materials, manufactured in Germany and invoiced at DM 600,000, payable at the end of January. The spot rate on 1 November was DM 2.50 per £, so the goods were entered into the books at £240,000. But what if sterling were to weaken, relative to the Deutschmark, to the point that the spot rate at the end of January reached DM 2.40 per £? Then it would cost £250,000 to buy the Deutschmarks with which to settle the invoice, ie an extra cost of £10,000;
- spent £210,000 on converting the materials into finished goods, which were despatched to the USA on 1 December, and invoiced at $720,000 dollars, due for payment at the end of January. The spot rate on 1 December was $1.5 per £, so the sale was booked at £480,000. But what if sterling were to strengthen relative to the dollar to the point that the spot rate at the end of January reached $1.6 per £? Then the dollars would be sold for only £450,000, ie a reduction in revenue of £30,000.

As far as accounting is concerned, the items had to be booked at the spot rate at the time the transaction was documented, ie when the material was received and when the goods were despatched, and a profit of £480,000 – £240,000 – £210,000, ie £30,000, recorded. If the company's year ended on 31 December, that would be the position shown in the accounts. In the event, the actual flows of cash would have been found to have been £450,000 – £250,000 – £210,000, ie a loss of £10,000.

Note how, as in this example, it is possible for one currency (sterling in this case) to weaken against another (the deutschmark) yet strengthen against a third (the dollar). It's all relative. Just as net short-term cash flows represent only a small proportion of the value of an entity, so its transaction risk is likely to represent only a small proportion of its total currency exposure. The bulk will normally be in the category called economic risk, to which we now turn.

## *ECONOMIC RISKS*

These are essentially the risks which affect a business before a transaction actually takes place, and are not, therefore, measurable in an accounting sense. They relate to the tactical and strategic levels of control, and are sometimes referred to as competitive risk.

Examples at the tactical level include such things as:

- insisting on dealing in only the home currency – sterling in the above example – thereby avoiding transaction risk, but opening up the risk that suppliers and customers will prefer to deal with competitors;
- deciding to increase the level of stock of an imported raw material, the world price of which (expressed in dollars) is expected to increase. This may well be borne out by events, but if sterling strengthens against the dollar in the meantime, competitors who did not increase their stock would buy their material more cheaply;
- entering into a competitive bidding process, in which it is necessary to quote a fixed price now, knowing that the buyer will not make a choice between suppliers for several weeks or even months;
- investing in a marketing campaign in, say, Spain, with a view to supplying goods or services in competition with local producers a few months hence. If sterling were to strengthen relative to the peseta, the appropriate peseta price might not convert into enough sterling to make it worth while;
- (equally important, but often overlooked) investing in a marketing campaign in, say, Spain, with a view to supplying

goods or services, in competition with French producers a few months hence. In this case, if the pound were to strengthen relative to the franc (even if both weakened against the peseta) a peseta price which appealed to the French supplier might not convert into enough sterling to make it worth while.

Examples at the strategic level include:

- deciding to acquire resources, say equipment in Italy, with a view to supplying goods or services to the UK market. If sterling were to weaken against the lira, the costs of the operation could become uneconomic;
- conversely, investing in plant in the UK to supply an overseas market. If sterling strengthens against the currency of the overseas country, the sterling conversion costs could render the business uneconomic;
- (possibly devastatingly, but again not widely appreciated) investing in the UK to supply the UK market, and not finding out until after the pound has strengthened against the rand that the same goods could then be supplied more cheaply from South Africa.

It is perhaps because these items do not appear in the accounts (because the business is lost to competitors) that they are less well understood. The fact is that, in today's conditions – as the last example showed – you do not even have to be importing or exporting to have an exposure to foreign currency risk. Identifying and quantifying (with inevitable margins of error) economic risk calls for a thorough appreciation of the competitive position and prospects of the enterprise. A proactive financial controller should be in the best position to carry out this task.

These economic risks affect potential rather than performance. A monitoring system based on forward-looking values could accommodate them, but one based on backward-looking costs cannot. This brings us to the question of the third category of risk, that associated with translation.

# TRANSLATION RISK

Translation risk does not affect the cash flows of the entity, but nevertheless attracts considerable treasury attention. It relates to the situation in which, for the purposes of preparing a balance sheet for publication, overseas assets and liabilities are translated at current rates into the currency of the country in which the entity is domiciled, eg into sterling for a UK-registered company. If sterling has weakened, overseas assets and liabilities will be translated into higher sterling figures; if sterling has strengthened, then they will be translated into smaller sterling figures.

Taking the first of these possibilities, let us imagine that a company borrows 10 million French francs, at a time when £1 is worth 10 francs. At that time, the borrowings would appear on the company's balance sheet at £1 million. Over the ensuing year, however, the pound falls in value to 8 francs; the borrowings would now be translated at £1.25 million, ie an apparent loss of £0.25 million. If this were assumed to be a permanent change in the pound–franc rate, it might be argued that this was a genuine loss of value, in the sense that more pounds would be needed to pay the interest and repay the loan in due course. The problem is that it is unreasonable to assume that the change is a permanent one. It could be reversed, reduced or increased in the next and subsequent years.

Meanwhile, the change in parity will have affected reported profits (and hence earnings per share) total assets, borrowings, net worth (and hence gearing) but as already mentioned it will not have affected the measured cash flow in the period being reported on. Academic theory argues that this risk, of itself, need not concern financial managers, but in practice there are two strong forces at work:

● although it does not affect the value of the entity as a whole, it can affect the attribution of that value as between the different stakeholders. Higher gearing may lead to higher interest rates being charged on bank loans, either directly in accordance with clauses in borrowing agreements or indirectly as a result of the company's credit rating being reduced. The banks benefit at the expense of the equity investors in the business. If the treasurer is pursuing an objective of maximizing the proportion of the value of the entity which accrues to the equity, he will want to manage this risk;

- if the accounts are being used 'beyond their design spec', eg as the basis for calculating bonus payments for directors and senior managers, then there is a temptation to protect the current year's figures, even though it is known that doing so has a long-term cost. This is comparable to pulling profit into the current year, knowing that it will both reduce next year's profit and result in tax being paid earlier than necessary.

The former is a good reason, the latter is often the real reason.

## POLITICAL RISK

Political risk is the unwanted consequences of political activities that will have an effect on the value of the firm. We are really only concerned with the detrimental effects. Examples of actions that can have a detrimental effect on the value of the firm are:

- discrimination against foreign businesses;
- expropriation of assets: expropriation involves the government confiscating private property; this may be done by nationalizing local subsidiaries;
- rules specifying use of local labour and materials;
- price-setting constraints;
- exchange controls; limitations on the extent to which a country's currency can be used to transfer funds or restrictions on the conversion of a currency into other currencies;
- tax regulations: an increase in the tax rate or introduction of new taxes;
- restrictions on access to local loans.

High political risk does not necessarily mean that a company should not invest in a particular country. It may be that the high political risk does not affect the firm's industry. Even if the project is affected by high political risk the level of returns available may be large enough to justify taking on the risk.

Liberalization of cross-border financial flows, coupled with technological developments which have speeded up and cheapened the costs of shifting funds around, have provided opportunities to protect against exchange rate and interest rate risks but, ironically, have opened up others which we may not have thought of before. The emergence of specialist managers (including those for hedge funds), and the growth in institutional investment abroad, have likewise added to liquidity in the market – but also added to instability.

The *daily* volume of trade in the foreign exchange markets is something like double the aggregate of national governments' reserves. The bulk represents speculative trading, driven by rumour, expectations, chartism, etc, and often national governments are put under pressure. Politicians try to resist market pressures but, by doing so, merely play into the hands of the speculators. The spot market, incidentally, now represents only a minority of the trade, thanks to the explosive growth of derivatives such as options and futures.

## *ATTITUDES TO RISK*

The examples quoted above tended to emphasize the downside risks, ie leading to an adverse effect on performance or potential. At this stage we need to recognize the upsides, too: if sterling weakens after you have invoiced in dollars, for example, your sterling income increases. This prompts the recognition of a spectrum of attitudes to risk, including:

- choosing to open up risks, ie to get into a position to benefit from exchange rate volatility, eg buying currencies which are expected to strengthen, writing options for other businesses. Perhaps only a small number of organizations are prepared to do this, but the high stakes mean that those which do need financial managers of the highest skill;

- accepting the risks which arise in the normal course of business as an inevitable element thereof, on a par with competitors discovering new ways of delivering the goods or services;

- taking a view on currency movements and finding a way to cover some (ie take some offsetting action) but not others. If you are confident that sterling can only weaken against the dollar, leave dollar receipts uncovered, but cover all payables, and vice versa. The basis for taking the view might be an econometric forecast, chartism or simply sentiment. As a general rule, however, confidence is misplaced at least as often as it is justified, as some embarrassing annual reports have shown;

- cover all identified risks in certain categories, eg all liabilities, all transaction exposures, all economic exposures included in the current 12-month forecast;

- hedge (ie cover a predetermined proportion of) identified exposures, eg 60 per cent of transaction risks, 40 per cent of economic risks included in the current 12-month forecast;

- matching opposite risks, eg those associated with importing and exporting – actively seeking matches by leading and lagging, perhaps, and covering or hedging only the net balance.

In organizational terms, there have been the usual debates as to whether currency risk management should be centralized or decentralized, and if the former, whether a profit centre or cost centre approach is appropriate. As time goes by, opinion seems to be hardening in favour of:

- decentralizing the responsibility for identifying risk;
- transferring identified risks to the centre at the market rate;

- giving (within defined limits) the centre discretion as to whether they actually take cover in the market;
- measuring their performance against the cost or benefit of covering everything at the market rate (ie they have to beat the market to be in credit).

Dealing with risk and individuals' attitudes to risk is vital to any decision-making process, and when multinationals look to evaluate investments overseas they have to compare the risks with the rewards.

## *SUMMARY*

In this chapter we have introduced some important foreign exchange terminology. We have identified the main types of foreign exchange risk which may have an impact on the method of financing overseas operations, analysed as transaction, translation, economic and political. The chapter concluded by considering different attitudes to risk and the trade-off between risk and reward.

# 9

# Exchange Risk Relationships

In the previous chapter we considered the main types of currency risk. In this chapter we identify the factors that cause a currency's value to change, both from a practical viewpoint and also by investigating a number of theoretical relationships which underpin a currency's exchange rate.

## PRACTICAL FACTORS AFFECTING EXCHANGE RATES

There are a number of factors that influence a currency's exchange rate:

- *Speculation*   A good example of how speculation can affect currency values occurred in 1992, when the UK government was forced to devalue sterling by the actions of speculators in the market who sold huge sums of sterling short (ie sold currency they did not own in the hope of buying it back more cheaply). The Bank of England was buying in the market in an attempt to maintain the value of sterling and base rates of interest were raised twice in one day. The speculators won, however. The UK withdrew from the European exchange rate mechanism and sterling was effectively devalued.
- *Balance of payments*   The net effect of importing and exporting will result in a demand or a supply for the country's currency.

- *Government policy* Governments from time to time may wish to change the value of their currency; this can be achieved directly by devaluation/revaluation or via the use of the 'foreign exchange markets'.

- *Interest rate differentials* A higher rate of interest can obviously create a demand for that particular currency, as people buy that currency in order to hold the currency with the higher interest rate.

- *Inflation rate differentials* Where countries have different inflation rates the value of one country's currency is reducing in 'real terms' in comparison with the other. This will result in a change in the exchange rate.

# THEORETICAL FOREX RELATIONSHIPS

Let us now consider a number of theoretical foreign exchange relationships which underpin changes in a currency's exchange rate.

## Interest rate parity (IRP)

Interest rates within a country are determined in the money market. The price of money, like anything else, is determined by supply and demand, although in many countries governments do try to manage the interest rate.

There is a strong relationship between the forex market and the money market. The relationship between the interest rates in two countries affects the rate of exchange, and in particular the relationship between the *spot rate of exchange* (ie the current rate at which a currency can be bought or sold, within a period of two days) and the *forward rate of exchange* (the rate being quoted for future transactions).

As identified above, there are many factors other than interest rates that affect movements in exchange rate over time. However, all things being equal, the currency with the higher interest rate will sell at a discount in the forward market against the currency with the lower interest rate. Or, to put it another way, if a country has a higher domestic rate of interest than its trading partner, it will find that this interest rate differential attracts foreign investors, and their desire to invest in that country will lead them to purchase the domestic currency, thus increasing that currency's spot rate.

However, assuming that the foreign investors will eventually wish to transfer their investment back into their own domestic currency, they will also engage in a forward contract. This is done at the same time as buying the foreign currency spot: they engage in a forward contract to convert the currency back into their own domestic currency, at some specified date in the future.

If, for example, the UK interest rate was 3 per cent higher than the US rate, in the spot transactions pounds would be *bought* and the spot rate for pounds would increase (as people wanted to take advantage of the higher rate of interest). But the pound would also be *sold* in the forward market, so the forward rate for the pound would be brought down. This is part of the speculator's process of arbitrage, that is, the simultaneous buying and selling of assets for a net gain.

The relationship between interest rates and the spot and forward rates can be expressed by a formula which uses interest rate differentials to calculate forward exchange rates for one period ahead:

$$\frac{r_\$ - r_\pounds}{1 + r_\pounds} = \frac{f_{\$/\pounds} - s_{\$/\pounds}}{s_{\$/\pounds}}$$

where

$r_\$$ and $r_\pounds$ = interest rate in dollars and pounds
$f_{\$/\pounds}$ = forward rate now
$s_{\$/\pounds}$ = spot rate now

Note $r_\$$ and $r_\pounds$ can be referred to as $i_F$ (interest rate in the foreign country) and $i_{UK}$ (interest rate in the UK).

This formula can be rearranged as follows:

$$\frac{1 + r_\$}{1 + r_£} = \frac{f_{\$/£}}{s_{\$/£}}$$

These points can best be illustrated by way of an example.

*Example*

Suppose that on 1 January 1995 the spot rate is £1 = $1.50 and the UK and US interest rates are 6 per cent and 8 per cent per annum respectively. What would we expect the one-year forward rate to be?

$$\frac{1 + r_\$}{1 + r_£} \times s_{\$/£} = f_{\$/£}$$

$$\frac{1 + 0.08}{1 + 0.06} \times 1.50 = 1.5283 \approx 1.53$$

*Proof*

$$\frac{0.08 - 0.06}{1.06} = \frac{1.5283 - 1.50}{1.50}$$

$$0.0189 = 0.0189$$

Now let us consider, in an attempt to explain the above theory, the sequence of events that would take place if someone in the UK was attracted by the high interest rate in the USA.

Assume that £100 was available for investment.

1.1.95
- Sell sterling and buy dollars
  £100 × 1.50 = $150
- Invest $150 for 12 months at 8%
  $150 × 8% = $12
- Total $ held ($150 + $12) = $162

31.12.95
- Sell dollars and buy back sterling
  $162/1.53 = £106

If however, the money had been left in the UK:

> 1.1.95      ●    Invest £100 for 12 months at 6%
>                       £100 × 6% = £6
> 31.12.95    ●    Total UK investment (£100 + £6) = £106

If the period is not 12 months, simply adjust the interest rate. For example, if the interest rate is quoted as 8 per cent per annum, and you are interested in the six months' forward rate, the interest rate to use is 8% × 6/12 = 4%.

### Example

Exporters plc, a UK company, is due to receive 500,000 Northland dollars in six months' time for goods supplied. The company decides to hedge its currency exposure by using the forward market. The short-term interest rate in the UK is 12 per cent per annum and the equivalent rate in Northland is 15 per cent. The spot rate of exchange is 2.5 Northland dollars to the pound.

### Required

Calculate how much Exporters plc actually gains or loses as a result of the hedging transaction if, at the end of six months, the pound, in relation to the Northland dollar, has (1) gained 4 per cent, (2) lost 2 per cent; or (3) remained stable. You may assume that the forward rate of exchange simply reflects the interest differential in the two countries (ie it reflects the interest rate parity analysis of forward rates).

### Solution

The forward rate can be calculated using the following formula:

$$\frac{1 + r_\$}{1 + r_£} \times s_{\$/£} = f_{\$/£}$$

The interest rates for six months are $15\% \times 6/12 = 0.075$ and $12\% \times 6/12 = 0.06$.

$$\frac{1.075}{1.06} \times \text{Nd } 2.50 = \text{Nd } 2.535$$

The exchange rate in six months' time is, therefore, Nd 2.535.

(1) If the spot rate strengthens by 4 per cent (ie from Nd 2.50 to Nd 2.60) then the company, had it secured the forward rate provided by the forward exchange market, would have saved £4,931 (£197,239 – £192,308).

Nd 500,000 ÷ 2.60 = £192,308
Nd 500,000 ÷ 2.535 = £197,239

(2) If the spot rate weakens by 2 per cent (ie from Nd 2.50 to Nd 2.45) then the company, had it secured the forward rate provided by the forward exchange market, would have lost £6,843 (£204,082 – £197,239).

Nd 500,000 ÷ 2.45 = £204,082

(3) If the spot rate remained unchanged at 2.50, then the company, had it secured the forward rate provided by the forward exchange market, would have lost £2,761 (£200,000 – £197,239).

## Purchasing power parity (PPP)

This alternative model suggests that, if the rate of inflation was, say, higher in country X than in country Y, then the rate of exchange of the currency of country X would fall against that of country Y.

One implication of this theory is that differences in inflation rates between countries will affect the movements in the exchange rate. The expected difference in the inflation rate would be expected to approximate to the expected change in the exchange rates. This relationship can best be illustrated by reference to the following formula:

$$\frac{i_F - i_{UK}}{1 + i_{UK}} = \frac{s_t - s_0}{s_0}$$

where

$i_F$ and $i_{UK}$ = inflation rate in the foreign country and the UK
$s_t$ = spot rate at a future time
$s_0$ = spot rate now

The formula can be rearranged to give a method of predicting future exchange rates.

$$\frac{1 + i_F}{1 + i_{UK}} \times s_0 = s_t$$

Consider the following example.

### Example

Bradbury cricket bats cost £100 in the UK and A$150 in Australia. The current exchange rate is A$1.50:£1. Explain what happens if inflation, which is presently 0 per cent in both the UK and Australia, increases to 10 per cent in Australia.

### Solution

The exchange rate becomes:

$$\frac{1 + 0.1}{1 + 0} \times 1.5 = 1.65$$

The cost of a bat in the UK remains at £100; in Australia it rises to A$165. This can also simply be shown by looking at the relative values of the goods as shown in Table 9.1.

**Table 9.1** Purchasing power parity

|  | UK | Australia | Exchange rate |
|---|---|---|---|
| Bats | £100 | A$150 | 150/100 = A$1.50 |
| Inflation | 0 (0%) | 15 (10%) | |
|  | £100 | A$165 | 165/100 = A$1.65 |

In reality, PPP – or the law of one price – does not hold, but comparing the price of an identical good in different countries allows study of the factors in those countries which might influence exchange rates and price differentials.

For some years, *The Economist* has published an annual index of purchasing power parity by reference to the price of 'Big Mac' hamburgers in McDonald's food outlets around the world. In the issue of 11 April 1998 the price of a Big Mac in the USA is quoted as $2.56, and in Germany as DM 4.95. The official exchange rate used in the article was DM 1.84. The exchange rate implied by the relative prices of Big Macs in the USA and Germany is DM 1.93 per US$ (4.95 ÷ 2.56). This implies that at this time, the Deutschmark was approximately 5 per cent overvalued against the dollar ((1.93 – 1.84) ÷ 1.84 × 100%).

The reasons for the big difference in price are likely to be market imperfections such as taxes, transaction costs, transport costs between markets, government intervention in exchange rates and McDonald's promotional activity in selected markets. However, over time the 'Big Mac Index' has been shown to be a useful predictor of exchange rates in the long term.

## The Fisher effect

The Fisher effect concentrates on the relationship between interest rates and inflation expectation between trading partners. Generally speaking, countries with higher rates of inflation will have higher nominal interest rates – both as a means of combating inflationary pressure and as a way of counteracting high inflation to provide investors with an adequate real rate of return. It is the second point which is stressed in the Fisher effect.

Why should the difference in interest rates equal the expected difference in inflation rates? In other words, why should the following formula hold good?

$$\frac{E(1 + i_\$)}{E(1 + i_£)} = \frac{1 + r_\$}{1 + r_£}$$

This is based on the basic Fisherian principle of interest rates that:

$$(1 + \text{real rate})(1 + \text{inflation rate}) = 1 + \text{money rate of interest}$$

For example, a building society may offer you a rate of interest of 6.09 per cent per year. If inflation is currently at 3 per cent per year, then the 'real' rate of interest you are receiving is 3 per cent $(1.0609/1.03 = 1.03)$. In other words, out of the 6.09 per cent interest rate you are receiving, 3 per cent protects you against inflation, and the remaining 3 per cent is the reward you get for investing your money for a year.

This principle also rests on the assumption that the expected real rate is the same in any two countries, ie the difference in money rates is the same as the expected difference in inflation rates; so the change in interest rates is determined by the expected change in inflation rates.

*Real* interest rates are more likely to be the same in the international eurocurrency markets than in the domestic capital markets. But any differences in real rates in different countries should not last very long. As people transfer holdings to foreign countries for higher real rates, *all* rates will be driven into equilibrium, so no one benefits. However, evidence has shown that the difference in interest rates *exaggerates* the likely differences in inflation rates, ie countries with high nominal interest rates also had relatively high real interest rates.

## *The International Fisher effect*

The International Fisher Effect holds that interest rate differentials should reflect the expected movement in the spot rate of exchange. The parity condition is derived from the two already discussed: namely, the PPP theory and the generalized Fisher Effect.

Countries that have higher interest rates than their trading partners are expected to experience currency depreciation, and hence the high interest rates are seen by foreign investors as a compensating payment for the future currency depreciation (because once depreciation occurs conversion of the foreign currency to the domestic currency will be lower). Countries with higher interest rates are starting from a higher base relative to countries with lower interest rates, and if capital is internationally mobile then it is believed that the real rate of return between countries will be equalized by the movements in the spot exchange rate in the appropriate direction. This means that interest rate differences between trading partners are offset by the spot exchange rate changing over time in the appropriate way.

For example, if the UK has 5 per cent higher interest rates than the USA, then to equalize the rates of return between the two nations, the pound should depreciate in value by a proportionate (5 per cent) amount against the dollar. This relationship can be shown as:

$$\frac{S_t}{S_0} = \frac{1 + r_{US}}{1 + r_{UK}}$$

where

$r_{US}$ and $r_{UK}$ = interest rate in dollars and pounds
$S_t$ = spot rate ($/£) at a future time
$S_0$ = spot rate ($/£) now

## *Expectations theory*

In the absence of risk, the expectations theory indicates that the percentage difference today between the forward rate and the spot rate is the change expected in the spot rate. The forward rate of exchange for, say, six months is what the spot rate is expected to be in six months' time, given expectations of interest rates and inflation.

Investors make estimates of the future spot rates of exchange, based on the current forward rate for the set time concerned, and then proceed to purchase and sell currencies accordingly. They purchase weak currencies (increase demand) which they expect to appreciate (become stronger) in the future; and they sell strong currencies (increase supply) which they expect to depreciate (become weaker) in the future. Their actions create a self-fulfilling prophecy, as the exchange rates are brought together on the basis of their actions. Weak currencies will appreciate under the buying pressure and strong currencies will depreciate under the selling pressure. Thus the action of speculators or hedgers is important in this area.

This 'expectations' hypothesis might not hold if investors think that future rates are risky or uncertain. For example, a company may have a requirement for dollars in the future, say in six months' time. They could wait until the end of the six months and then buy dollars, but this leaves them open to the risk that the price of dollars will go up. Here, it is safer to buy the dollars forward and these people will, therefore, be prepared to buy forward even if the price of dollars is a little higher than the expected spot rate. The opposite may happen with a company which is expecting to receive dollars in the future, ie they may be prepared to sell forward even if the price of dollars is a little lower than the expected spot rate. So, depending on which type of investors predominate, we may see:

Forward rate $\leq$ expected future spot rate

In fact, the empirical evidence on this shows that, at any one point in time, we may see the forward rate higher than the expected future spot rate and lower at other times. But for this theory to hold in practice, it is only necessary for the two rates to be equal *on average* over time, and, again, there is much evidence to support this averaging effect. In connection with this the results have shown that it is extremely difficult to *predict* future spot rates given the forward rate. For example, if the forward rate is less than today's spot rate, the odds are only a little better than evens that the spot rate will increase in the future. Therefore, we can use these and other relationships presented to predict in broad terms what will happen in the long run to exchange rates, but short-term changes are more difficult to forecast.

### *Implications of these theories*

Two of these theories, interest rate parity and purchasing power parity, rely heavily on arbitrage arguments. These theories must hold if there are a large number of quick-acting buyers and sellers and small transaction costs.

The other three involve views about risk. They do not hold if investors agree that one currency or country is riskier than the other. However, we can safely use (on average over a period of time!) *forward rates to tell us how to allow for exchange rate risk* (ie whether future spot rates will increase or decrease).

Although exchange rates do, to some extent, and in the long run, adjust for differences in inflation rates and nominal interest rates, sometimes they do not, so it is definitely worth while to try to *combat exchange rate risk* when considering foreign currency investment or borrowing in any shape or form.

## *SUMMARY*

The theoretical foreign exchange relationships that we have considered in this chapter are important, as they help to explain why exchange rates between currencies tend to change. Once the reasons for exchange rate movement have been identified, foreign exchange risks can be fully understood and techniques to hedge these risks may be developed. These hedging techniques are covered in the next chapter.

# 10

# Currency Risk Management

In Chapter 8 we identified the types of risk associated with over-seas trading. In this chapter we look at methods suitable for hedging these risks. The techniques for hedging currency risk are many and varied. Most are aimed at hedging transaction risks, although some are also useful for hedging translation risks. We begin with a brief reminder of transaction risk before considering a number of hedging techniques.

## TRANSACTION RISK

Transaction risk occurs when there is a time delay between the sale of goods and the receipt of the payments, and it will occur in all foreign trading. The question is: who bears the risk?

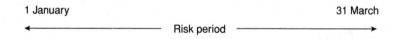

1 January           31 March
◄──────────────── Risk period ──────────────►

**Figure 10.1** Transaction risk

If the spot rate was £1 = US $1.50 and £1,500-worth of goods were sold on 1 January, the risk period is the three months to 31 March as illustrated in Figure 10.1. The exchange rate could move to £1 = $2, thus changing the sterling value received from £1,000 (1,500/1.50) to £750 (1,500/2.00), a loss of £250.

The businesspeople exposed to transaction risk can either run the risk of exchange rate movements or they can take steps to protect their future cash flows from exchange rate fluctuation. If they have sold goods abroad and are prepared to gamble they could, in addition to the profit on the sale of the goods, find that they have made a currency gain. This would happen if the rate of exchange had moved in their favour between the time that they delivered the goods and the time they are paid. However, it could be that the rate of exchange moves the other way, giving them a currency loss (as indicated above) and perhaps meaning that the payments they receive when converted into their own currency do not cover their costs. It is to avoid this possibility that many businesspeople seek to avoid the risks of currency movements by hedging.

Once an enterprise has decided to hedge a particular foreign currency risk, there are a number of methods to consider. They have been grouped here under the following headings:

- internal/traditional hedging techniques;
- forward markets and money market hedge;
- futures;
- options.

## INTERNAL/TRADITIONAL HEDGING TECHNIQUES

### Invoicing in sterling

Here the company simply invoices in its own currency. The risk is not avoided here, it is merely transferred to the customer. This technique may not always be possible, given that the company may well be competing with local industries invoicing in the local currency, and as such, the overseas quote may become uncompetitive.

## Multilateral netting

This is a form of matching appropriate for multinational groups or companies with subsidiaries or branches in a number of overseas countries. The process is based on determining a base currency, eg £ sterling or US dollars, so that the intra-group transactions are recorded only in that currency; each group company reports its obligations to other group companies to a central, say UK, treasury department, which then informs each subsidiary of the net receipt or payment needed to settle their foreign exchange intra-group positions.

While this procedure undoubtedly reduces transaction costs by reducing the number of transactions and also reduces exchange rate risk by reducing currency flows, the difficulties are that there are regulations in certain countries which severely limit or even prohibit netting, and there may also be cross-border legal and taxation problems to overcome as well as the extra administrative costs of the centralized treasury operation.

### Example

A group of companies controlled from the UK includes subsidiaries in Belgium, France and the USA. It is forecast that, at the end of the month, intercompany indebtedness will be as follows:

- The Belgian subsidiary will be owed BF144,381,000 by the French subsidiary and will owe the US subsidiary US$1,060,070.
- The French subsidiary will be owed FF14,438,000 by the US subsidiary and will owe it US$800,000.

It is a function of the central treasury department to net-off intercompany balances as far as possible and to issue instructions for settlement of the net balances. For this purpose, the relevant exchange rates in terms of £1 are $1.415; FF10.215; BF68.10.

## *Required*

Calculate the net payments to be made in respect of the above balances. The scenario is shown diagrammatically in Figure 10.2.

## *Solution*

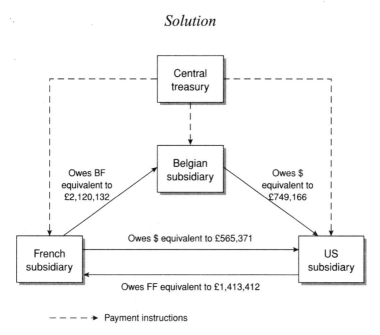

Figure caption labels:
- Central treasury
- Belgian subsidiary
- French subsidiary
- US subsidiary
- Owes BF equivalent to £2,120,132
- Owes $ equivalent to £749,166
- Owes $ equivalent to £565,371
- Owes FF equivalent to £1,413,412
- – – – → Payment instructions

**Figure 10.2** Multilateral netting

First set out Table 10.1 in the separate currencies.

**Table 10.1** Inter-company balances in currency

|  | *Belgium* | *France* | *USA* |
|---|---|---|---|
| Belgium | – | BF144,381,000 | ($1,060,070) |
| France | (BF144,381,000) | – | FF14,438,000 |
|  |  |  | ($800,000) |
| USA | $1,060,070 | (FF14,438,000) |  |
|  |  | $800,000 |  |

Now convert Table 10.2 to £ sterling.

**Table 10.2** Inter-company balances in sterling

|  | Belgium | France | USA | Total |
|---|---|---|---|---|
| Belgium | – | 2,120,132 | (749,166) | 1,370,966 |
| France | (2,120,132) | – | 1,413,412 | (1,272,091) |
|  |  |  | (565,371) |  |
| USA | 749,166 | (1,413,412) | – | (98,875) |
|  |  | 565,371 |  |  |

Central treasury department will instruct the French subsidiary to pay the Belgian subsidiary £1,272,091, and the US subsidiary to pay the Belgian subsidiary £98,875. Possible advantages of this procedure are:

- lower transaction costs as a result of fewer transactions;
- regular settlements may reduce intra-company exposure risks.

Possible disadvantages are that:

- if the base currency is generally weak against other currencies for a sustained period, subsidiary company results could be significantly distorted;
- if a particular subsidiary is suffering from cash-flow problems, the centre may have to arrange for it to have additional funds for settlements, thereby offsetting some or all of the transaction cost benefits and possibly incurring exchange losses;
- the central treasury may have difficulties in exercising the strict control that the procedure demands;
- tax considerations may be adverse.

This is known as multilateral netting. If it involved only two companies it would be referred to as bilateral netting.

## Leading and lagging

This method involves changing the timing of payments in an attempt to take advantage of changes in the relative value of the currencies involved. *Leading* is making payments in advance of the due date whereas *lagging* is delaying payments until after the due date. If a company feels that it can reasonably predict the direction of exchange-rate changes, then:

- If the company has a debtor, ie an asset, in a currency predicted to depreciate, it should aim to dispose of this asset as soon as possible. This is the process of 'leading'.
- If, however, it has a creditor, ie a liability, in a currency predicted to depreciate, then it should aim to delay payment for as long as possible. This is the process of 'lagging'.
- If the currency involved is strong or appreciating the company should 'lag' its receipts and 'lead' its payments.

Of course, a 'lead' payment can involve a cost in terms of interest forgone.

### Example

Suppose you have to pay a US supplier US$200,000 in one month's time and the forward rate and spot rates are 1.4255 and 1.4295 respectively. There are a number of options available:

*Forward contract*   If you entered into a forward contract to buy dollars, the amount that you would have to pay in a month's time would be:

Forward rate = 1.4255   spot rate = 1.4295
200,000/1.4255 = £140,301.65

*Spot in one month*   Alternatively, you could wait for a month and convert at the prevailing spot price. If the forward contracts are the best estimate of future spot rates then the amount payable would be the same as above, ie £140,301.65.

*Lead payment*   The third possibility is to make a lead payment – settle the amount now. This will cost you:

200,000/1.4295 = £139,909.06

If interest payments are ignored the lead payment proves the cheapest method.

## Matching

This is the use of receipts in a particular currency to match payment obligations in the same currency.

A UK company may have a substantial trade with another country overseas, involving both debtor and creditor transactions, eg where goods are exported and invoiced in a foreign currency and the overseas sales transacted are also paid for in that currency. The UK company may well benefit from operating a foreign currency account, whereby its exchange risk is limited to any conversions of the net account balance into sterling. A further advantage is that balances on the account can be cleared, ie disposed of, if the exchange rate is favourable to the account-holder.

The foreign currency account can either be held with a domestic bank, eg in the UK, or by using, say, a bank deposit account in the overseas country. Note that UK residents are permitted to hold bank accounts in respect of any foreign currency.

If there are likely to be significant balances on the account, or frequent remittances to the UK, the account-holder may well need exchange risk protection by taking out some form of hedging cover.

Matching is more commonly found in multinational group situations, where different subsidiary companies intertrade. Matching is also a technique that may be used to hedge translation risks.

If a UK company has an investment in assets in the USA, exposure to movements in the exchange rate between sterling and the

US dollar can be reduced by financing the investment with a US dollar loan; if the exchange rate alters, the change in the sterling value of the asset will be matched by a corresponding change in the sterling value of the US dollar loan. For example, a company may purchase a factory unit in the USA for US$400,000, financing the purchase by means of a loan denominated in dollars.

## HEDGING USING THE FINANCIAL MARKETS

### Forward markets

A forward contract is one in which one party agrees to buy 'something', and another party agrees to sell that same 'something' at a designated date in the future. For example, in the case of a forward exchange contract, one party agrees to deliver a specified amount of one currency for another at a specified exchange rate at a designated date in the future. The specified exchange rate is called the *forward rate*. The designated date at which the parties must transact is called the *settlement date* or *delivery date*.

When an investor takes a position in the market by buying a forward contract, the investor is said to be in a *long position*. If, instead, the investor's opening position is the sale of a forward contract, the investor is said to be in a *short position*.

The foreign exchange forward market is an interbank market. Most forward contracts have a maturity of less than two years. For longer-dated forward contracts, the bid–ask spread increases; that is, the size of the spread for a given currency increases with the maturity. Consequently, forward contracts become less attractive for hedging long-dated foreign currency exposure.

### Forward exchange fixed contract

A forward exchange contract is an agreement, entered into today, to purchase or sell a fixed quantity of a commodity, currency or other financial instrument on a fixed future date at a price fixed today. They are tailor-made to meet the exact requirements of the contract, and once entered into, the contract must be completed. A major problem with a forward contract is the fixed settlement date. By using an option forward contract this can be overcome.

### *Forward exchange option contract*

A forward exchange option contract offers the same arrangement as a forward contract except that there is a choice of dates on which the user can exercise the contract. This is either on any date up to a specified date or at any time between two future dates. In either case the forward rate that applies would be the forward rate, in the period in which the contract can be exercised, that is *least favourable* to the purchaser of the contract.

### *Example*

The Kidwelly Sweetie Company exports confectionery to a number of department stores in the USA and Europe. It is due to receive US$12,000 in six months' time from goods supplied to a US customer.

The six-month US dollar forward rate is 1.4550–1.4600.

The spot rate is 1.4960–1.4990.

Calculate the sterling receipt if the company decides to hedge using a forward exchange contract.

### *Solution*

When deciding which rate to use, it will always be the one that gives the lower sterling value for receipts and the highest sterling value for payments.

$$\frac{\$12,000}{1.4550} = £8,247 \qquad \frac{\$12,000}{1.4600} = £8,219$$

Therefore, the sterling receipt is £8,219, as this is the lower of the two.

## *Problems with forward contracts*

Note that a forward exchange contract is binding. If, for example, importers discover eventually that they have contracted to buy more currency than they need to pay their suppliers, they are required to take up the full contractual amount at the agreed forward rate. They can then sell back any surplus to the bank at the spot rate on the day they settle. This is known as 'closing out' the contract. Similarly, exporters who have contracted to sell forward more currency than they actually receive from their customers will be required to buy extra amounts at spot in order to close out their contracts.

## *Money market hedge*

The use of the forward market as a 'hedge' against variations in exchange rates was illustrated above. Using the forward market it was possible to ensure that the exchange rate applying at some future date was known with certainty. Another way of achieving this is to use the money market. More steps are involved, and they are illustrated below.

## *Example*

Details are the same as the example above, with the following additional information on interest rates:

|       | *Borrow* | *Lend* |
|-------|----------|--------|
| USA   | 12%      | –      |
| UK    | –        | 10%    |

*Solution*

1.  Borrow from the bank at the discounted value.

$$\frac{\$12,000}{1.06*} = \$11,320$$

* $\frac{12\%}{2}$ for six months only

The amount borrowed will then compound up to US$12,000 in six months' time and can be paid off by the receipt of US$12,000 from the US customer.

2.  Convert at the sterling spot rate.

$$\frac{11,320}{1.4990} \simeq £7,552$$

3.  Invest at the sterling interest rate.

$$7,552 \times 1.05* \simeq £7,930$$

*$\frac{10\%}{2}$ for six months only

This is only necessary so that comparisons can be made with forward exchange contracts. This amount is less than the forward exchange contract, therefore, the company should hedge using the forward exchange contract, and receive £8,219.

In reality, the money may well be invested elsewhere within the business, or used to pay off outstanding liabilities.

## SELECTING A HEDGING METHOD

When a company has an outstanding foreign currency payable or receivable, it may choose to hedge against the currency risk by using the forward markets or the money markets. The method selected should be the one which leads to the smallest payment in sterling terms, or the highest receivable in sterling terms.

*Example*

LMN plc exports its products throughout the world. It has today received from a regular customer in France an order worth £350,000 at today's spot market exchange rate. It has also received from a new customer in Uganda an order worth £150,000 at today's spot rate. Both orders are to be paid in the respective importer's currency. Terms of trade are 60 days' credit. No discount is offered for early payment. Experience has shown that the French customer may take up to 90 days to pay. Exchange rates and money market rates are shown in Tables 10.3 and 10.4.

These rates are fixed for a period of two or three months for immediate deposits or borrowings. LMN plc converts all foreign currency receipts into sterling immediately on receipt. Wherever possible, the company uses forward exchange contracts to hedge its currency risks.

In view of the lack of forward markets in Uganda, the Ugandan customer has offered to pay US$225,000 to LMN plc in three months' time instead of Ugandan shillings in 60 days. The customer

**Table 10.3** Foreign exchange rates (mid rates)

|  | *FF/US$* | *US$/£* | *Uganda shillings/£* |
|---|---|---|---|
| Spot | 5.7485 | 1.4920 | 1,700 |
| 1 month forward | 5.7622 | 1.4898 | N/A |
| 2 months forward | 5.7727 | 1.4886 | |
| 3 months forward | 5.7833 | 1.4873 | |

**Table 10.4** Money market rates (% per annum)

|  | *Deposit* | *Borrowing* |
|---|---|---|
| UK bank | 5 | 8 |
| Uganda bank | 15 | N/A |
| US domestic bank | 3 | 6 |

is able to do this as a result of his government's new economic liberalization policies. Using the above data we are able to:

1.  calculate the sterling receipts that LMN plc can expect from its sales to the French customer, assuming LMN plc hedges its risk using the forward market;
2.  calculate the expected sterling receipts from the Ugandan customer, assuming its offer of payment in US dollars is accepted. Assume LMN plc hedges its risk using:
    *   the forward market; or
    *   the money market;
    and advise LMN plc on which method is most advantageous;
    *   advise LMN plc on whether the Ugandan customer's offer of payment in US dollars should be accepted.

### Solution

1.  The exchange rates between sterling and the French franc can be calculated as follows:

Spot   8.5768   2 months   8.5932   3 months   8.6015

The value of the first order is FF350,000 × 8.5768, ie FF3,001,880. The forward contract appropriate to the situation described would be an option one, ie for completion between 60 and 90 days. This would be priced at 8.6015, to yield FF3,001,880/8.6015, ie £348,995.

2.  *   The Uganda order is worth US$225,000 in three months' time. This could be sold forward at 1.4873, to yield £151,281.
    *   Alternatively, the exporter could borrow US$221,675 and pay interest of US$3,325, the total being repaid when the US$225,000 is received from Uganda. The US$221,675 would be worth £148,575 on which interest of £1,857 would be earnt, bringing the total to £150,432.

On this basis, use of the forward exchange rate is the more beneficial.

- Purely in terms of exchange rate risk, the exporter would be advised to accept the US dollar arrangement. This being a new customer, however, in a part of the world going through significant change, there may well be credit and political risks. The exporter should quantify these, and weigh them against the profitability of the product.

## *FUTURES*

Financial futures in foreign exchange rates are contracts to buy or sell an amount of foreign currency at a future date, and are traded on futures exchanges such as the Chicago Mercantile Exchange, which has a London office. The futures exchange quotes a price for each contract on every trading day, so that contracts are saleable before their delivery date. Although this makes them flexible, there are restrictions in that contracts have to be for specific amounts of currency (eg £25,000 blocks for a currency future against the US dollar) and delivery dates are limited.

### *Example*

A UK company Clark plc sells goods to Smith Inc in the USA to the value of US$2,650,000. The sale takes place in June with payment due in August. The finance director of Clark plc is concerned that the pound will strengthen against the dollar which would reduce the sterling value of the contract. The spot rate in June is US$1.5050/£.

Assume that in June a September dollar/pound futures contract is quoted at US$1.5000. This means that the futures market will buy or sell pounds for dollars for future delivery, in September, at an exchange rate of US$1.5000/£.

To hedge against the risk of the £ strengthening against the dollar, Clark plc would need to buy an appropriate number of dollars/pounds futures contracts. This means that Clark plc has agreed to buy pounds for dollars on the future delivery date at the exchange rate specified by the price of the futures contract. The sterling futures contracts which are traded on the Chicago Mercantile Exchange (CME) are for £62,500.

The number of contracts that Clark plc would need to buy is:

$$\$2,650,000 \div 1.5000 = £1,766,667 \div £62,500 = 28.27$$
$$\text{contracts}$$

Only a whole number of contracts can be traded, so Clark plc would need to buy either 28 or 29 contracts. We shall assume 28 contracts, although this will leave a small amount unhedged.

In August, just before Smith Inc is due to pay, the futures contract price has changed to US$1.5200 and the spot rate has also moved to US$1.5200/£. Clark plc will now close out its position in the futures contracts by selling the futures contracts.

|  | $ |
|---|---|
| Profit on futures | |
| $(1.5200 - 1.5000) \times 62,500 =$ | |
| $1,250 per contract × 28 contracts | 35,000 |
| Received from Smith Inc | 2,650,000 |
| | 2,685,000 |

The total receipts of US$2,685,000 will be sold on the spot market to give a sterling receipt of $2,685,000/1.5200 = £1,766,447$ and an effective exchange rate for the US$2,650,000 received of $2,650,000/1,766,447 = US\$1.5002$.

In practice, the profit on the futures contracts would be received as it arose during the period from June to August. Note also that if the pound had weakened against the dollar, a loss would have been made on the futures contract, but this would have been offset by receiving more pounds in the spot market in August.

# *OPTIONS*

Options give the client the right – but not the obligation – to buy ('call') or sell ('put') a specific amount of currency at a specific price on a specific date. The banks take into account the costs of buying and selling currencies and the potential profits, and distil them all into the premium payable for the option. The level of premium depends on a number of factors:

- the strike price. This might be:
  - 'at the money', ie the agreed price corresponds with that currently available (spot or forward);
  - 'in the money', ie the agreed price is more favourable to the client than is currently available (but then the premium would be higher);
  - 'out of the money', ie the price is less favourable to the client than is currently available (but then the premium would be low – possibly zero);
- the maturity: the premium follows the line of a diminishing returns curve, eg a six-month option will not be twice as expensive as a three-month option;
- the volatility of the spot rate, ie the greater the volatility, the greater the premium;
- interest rate differentials, which affect the banks' carrying costs;
- liquidity in the market, sentiment and other judgemental factors.

### *Example*

A company is tendering for the sale of equipment to a US company for $3 million, settlement due in three months' time. The current spot rate is US$1.58:£1. However, the company is worried about the dollar weakening against the pound, thus making the sale less profitable.

The company has been offered a three-month put option on US dollars at US$1.60:£1, costing 0.02 cents per pound. What is the company's position?

*Solution*

The sterling amount received if the option is exercised:

$$\frac{\$3\ \text{million}}{\$1.60} = £1,875,000$$

In addition, the cost of the option itself must be considered. This is quoted in cost per foreign currency unit:

$$0.02\ \text{cents} \times £1,875,000 = \$37,500$$

This is payable regardless of whether the option itself is exercised. Hence the net sterling amount:

|  | | [£] |
|---|---|---|
| To sell $3 million | | 1,875,000 |
| Cost of option (at spot) | $\dfrac{\$37,500}{\$1.58}$ | (23,734) |
| | | 1,851,266 |

Clearly, the advantage here is that if the spot rate moves in the company's favour (say, to US$1.54) then the option can be abandoned and the dollars sold on the spot market. Secondly, if the tender is not won, the company has no binding obligation to deliver dollars in three months' time.

Observation suggests that the option route is becoming increasingly popular. It sits comfortably alongside a situation in which the cash flows themselves are subject to considerable uncertainty, eg the tactical component of economic risk. If you cannot be sure the dollars will be received, you do not want to be committed to delivering them to the bank at a fixed price!

There are rules and products to deal with delays in currency becoming available and, of course, the options have a (positive or negative) value at a point in time. This can be left unrealized, or could be realized by selling the option or taking up an opposing position in the market. The scope for switching profit between accounting periods is enormous.

There are various other products available on the futures markets, and there are various combinations of these products, called derivatives. You can, for example, get a lower cost, or even zero cost, option by agreeing to forgo some of the 'upside' potential or take some of the 'downside' risk. There are caps, floors, collars and swap agreements. These derivatives can be extremely important in financial management, but the above is probably sufficient to introduce the products and their underlying logic. Selection and monitoring in this area has become a very specialized skill, given the need to be aware of developments, not only of new instruments, but also of the security of the company writing them.

Many banks seized the opportunity to diversify into these products as their core credit intermediation businesses were going through difficult times, and capital adequacy ratios were being tightened. They and the regulators are not sure that they fully understand the products and are able to manage this level of complexity. Likewise, there are some concerns regarding the rapid spread of computerized trading systems and the increasing interdependence of markets: problems in one area could easily spread to others. It does not help that the legal and taxation framework has not been able to keep pace.

## *SUMMARY*

This chapter has considered a range of potential techniques for hedging foreign currency risk. Most of these are aimed at hedging transaction risks, but the technique of matching may equally be used to hedge transaction or translation risk.

Treasury managers need to be aware of the range of hedging techniques available to them and the relative attractions of each. Important considerations in the selection of an appropriate hedging technique will be cost, flexibility, ease of administration and attitude to risk.

# References

Brealey, R, Myers, S C and Marcus, S (1996) *Fundamentals of Corporate Finance*, McGraw-Hill, Maidenhead

## *FURTHER READING*

Baumol, W J (1952) The transactions demand for cash: an inventory theoretic approach, *Quarterly Journal of Economics*, November

Miller, M N and Orr, D (1966) A model of the demand for money by firms, *Quarterly Journal of Economics*, August

Modigliani, F and Miller, M H (1958) The cost of capital, corporation finance and the theory of investment, *American Economic Review*, **48**, 26–96

Modigliani, F and Miller, M H (1963) Taxes and the cost of capital: a correction, *American Economic Review*, **53**, 433–43

# Index

# Visit Kogan Page on-line

Comprehensive information on
Kogan Page titles

## Features include

- complete catalogue listings,
  including book reviews and
  descriptions

- special monthly promotions

- information on NEW titles and
  BESTSELLING titles

- a secure shopping basket facility
  for on-line ordering

PLUS everything you need to know
about KOGAN PAGE

# http://www.kogan-page.co.uk